WEDDING
INSPIRATIONS

Margaret Caselton

text by Antonia Swinson

WEDDING
INSPIRATIONS

stylish ways to create a perfect day

RYLAND
PETERS
& SMALL
LONDON NEW YORK

photography by Polly Wreford

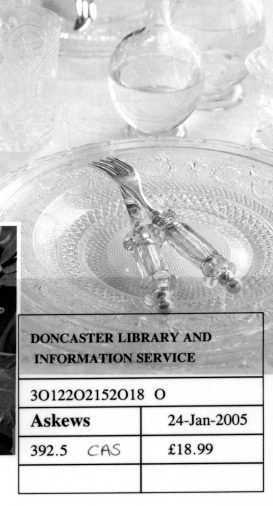

To my dear friend Sandy Boler, *MC*

Senior designer Catherine Griffin
Senior editor Annabel Morgan
Location research Claire Hector
Production manager Patricia Harrington
Art director Gabriella Le Grazie
Publishing director Alison Starling

Stylist Margaret Caselton
Text Antonia Swinson

First published in the United Kingdom
in 2005 by Ryland Peters & Small
20–21 Jockey's Fields
London WC1R 4BW
www.rylandpeters.com

10 9 8 7 6 5 4 3 2 1

Text, design and photographs
© Ryland Peters & Small 2005

ISBN 1 84172 791 1

Printed and bound in China

contents

THIS PAGE: *An idyllic scene awaits guests: a loggia overlooking a country garden is the backdrop for white tables set with colourful flowers, fine crystal and floral china.*

I love weddings. They are such an affirmation of hope for the future. They are also the perfect opportunity for friends and family to celebrate the joy and happiness of the couple. And at the reception, the bride and groom can express their gratitude and affection by giving their guests a party to remember.

This book is for everybody who has a wedding to look forward to. It is a book of ideas for you to adapt to suit your own particular style and theme. The book begins with a chapter on planning to point you in the right direction. There follows sections on different wedding styles to demonstrate how to combine decorative elements to produce a finished look that's coordinated and stylish, but still personal. Chapters on separate elements follow: bridal flowers and floral decorations; confetti; cakes; table settings; favours; and candles. Attention to detail makes all the difference, and it's often the little things that create the biggest impression.

The book is designed to inspire, so pick and mix the things that suit you and your wedding. It's a compliment to everyone who attends your wedding to make the day as beautiful as it can be. Most importantly, have fun, both during the planning and, above all, on the day!

Margaret Caselton

a day to remember...

FAR LEFT: *Delicate floral detail on the china reinforces a colour scheme of soft pinks and plums.*
LEFT: *A diaphanous purple ribbon tied into a large bow round a wineglass stem is a simple but striking touch.*
ABOVE: *A table centrepiece contrasts white stephanotis with ruby red carnations, making a dramatic and sophisticated statement.*

planning

PLANNING A WEDDING IS AN EXCITING BUT INTIMIDATING PROSPECT, SO GOOD ORGANIZATION IS ABSOLUTELY VITAL. ONCE YOU'VE SET THE DATE, START COLLECTING ANYTHING THAT INSPIRES YOU, THEN SET ABOUT TURNING YOUR DREAMS INTO REALITY...

GATHERING INSPIRATION

Organizing a wedding involves many decisions and lots of elements – the
dress, flowers, cake, food, decorations and so on. Having a clear sense of
what you want to achieve before you start is the best way to avoid a result that
looks ill-conceived or thrown together. So planning time is never wasted time.
Putting in the thought and groundwork months before the big day is essential if
you want your vision to become reality.

   This doesn't mean that stylish weddings must be elaborate and expensive.
Far from it. If yours is an informal country wedding, jam jars overflowing with

wild flowers would be fabulous table centrepieces. However, even this look of rustic simplicity needs to be carefully followed through, right down to the last favour, if it is to be a success. Planning early allows you time to explore different options and shop around. It also gives you the chance to start again if something doesn't work out the way you wanted.

One of the best ways to get the ball rolling is to start collecting things that capture something of the look you're after. You might end up with pictures from magazines, scraps of fabric, paint charts, ribbons, flowers, even inspirational words or phrases. Pin up a length of string on a wall or the side of a cupboard, and peg your objects along it. Then live with them for a week and see how the items work together, how well the colours complement each other and whether

OPPOSITE AND ABOVE:
Putting up a piece of string and pegging objects to it, just as you would washing, is one way of building up a collection of items that inspire you and sum up the look you want to achieve at your wedding.
RIGHT: *Another approach is to create a mood board, much in the way that fashion designers do, pinning up your sources of inspiration so that you can live with them and see how they work together before making any final decisions.*

Did you know THAT THE EGYPTIANS ARE THOUGHT
TO HAVE BEGUN THE PRACTICE OF WEARING A RING ON THE THIRD
FINGER OF THE LEFT HAND, BECAUSE THEY BELIEVED THAT THE
VEIN IN THIS FINGER RAN STRAIGHT TO THE HEART?

a coherent picture is emerging. On similar lines, you could pin everything up to
make a mood board. Either way, these visual aides-mémoire are an easy and
effective way to clarify your ideas and find out what works and what doesn't.
Choosing a reception venue will be an early, and crucial, decision. Make sure
that the style you're striving for will sit easily in its surroundings. As our four
styles of wedding show (see pages 14–29), working with a location, and never
against it, is the way to achieve a beautiful result.

Finally, remember that however complicated an organizational task a wedding
is, it should be a pleasure, not a burden. Enjoy planning the event of a lifetime
and don't lose sight of what's at the heart of it all – the solemnization of a
loving union and the celebration of a new chapter in your life.

OPPOSITE: *Before ordering your
invitations, collect examples of paper, fonts
and inks. Your wedding stationery will be the
first indication your guests receive of the
type of day you're planning.*

ABOVE: *Suspension files are a good way
of organizing your wedding paperwork.
Make sure they're colourful rather than
purely utilitarian, so that they remind you of
fun rather than work.*

LEFT: *Attractive albums are another way
of collecting ideas. Slip cuttings, swatches
and pictures within their pages, and turn
them into keepsakes after the wedding's over.*

LEFT: *The bride's ensemble is, like the setting, elegant, streamlined and simple.*
BELOW LEFT: *To display place cards unfussily in such a minimalist tablescape, they are tucked inside the wineglasses.*
RIGHT: *Tall, tapered vases hold two towering stems of agapanthus in a display of almost Oriental austerity. Stainless-steel and glass candle holders add a softening note of warmth, but everything about the table setting is pared down and pure.*

MODERN WEDDING

A location as strikingly architectural and uncompromisingly modern as this one cries out for an equally minimalist style of reception. An all-white colour scheme is the obvious choice, successfully combining simplicity with romance. For the table setting, white china has been partnered with plain silver cutlery, glass votives and vases, and etched glassware. Tradition has not been dispensed with altogether – there are white damask napkins and a three-tiered wedding cake – but the whole affair has been approached in a spirit of simplicity. Nor has nature been forgotten: there are flowers, shells and an emphasis on circles and curves in the table setting. The white-on-white theme produces a serene look that is prevented from tipping over into the clinical by the spectacular view over the lake to the lush trees beyond.

The top table dominates the room, with white chairs inspired by Arne Jacobsen's Series 7 neatly lined up down one side. When a table setting is as simple as this one, the elements need to be selected and arranged with great care. Here, even the chairs have been placed so that they form a perfectly straight line. Slender glass vases holding two agapanthus

THIS PAGE: *The top table is positioned to offer a view of the bridal couple set against a backdrop of water, trees and sky. The colour scheme is all white, and every element of the table setting has been laid out with exacting precision.*

THIS PAGE: *In keeping with the precision and formality of the table setting, the chairs are lined up down one side of the top table. In the background, the cake sits on a long, white shelf.*

OPPOSITE, ABOVE: *Despite the austerity of the setting, there is softness here, too. Etched glasses and spiralling shells contribute a subtle theme of circles, while the napkins are thick, luxurious damask.*

stems are set at every third place setting, and the stainless-steel candle holders sit to the top left of each plate at even intervals. Such precision creates a rhythm and pattern that is responsible for the success of this look. In a sparsely set tablescape it is also vital that the items used have an elegance and beauty of form. Here, a subtle theme of circles runs throughout, thanks to the etched glasses, grooved plates and gleaming shells that sit on top of each napkin. The cake, too, nods to the circle motif, with its decoration of icing 'pearls', graduating from large to small on each tier. Without these careful details, the table would be in danger of looking too austere. It is important that among sleek, hard-edged materials there are softening touches. The delicate blooms, flickering nightlights and heart-shaped ice cubes in the chunky glass ice buckets all serve as reminders that this is, after all, a wedding.

Did you know THAT IN THE MIDDLE AGES A WHITE WEDDING CAKE WAS PRIZED NOT AS A SYMBOL OF THE BRIDE'S PURITY BUT OF HER FAMILY'S WEALTH? THE PURER AND WHITER THE SUGAR USED IN THE ICING, THE MORE EXPENSIVE THE CAKE.

RIGHT: *The wedding cake combines tradition and modernity. Its three tiers are decorated with ever-decreasing opalescent icing 'pearls' and it is topped with a cluster of immaculate eucharis lilies.*
FAR RIGHT: *A champagne bottle sits chilling in a glass bucket filled with heart-shaped ice cubes.*

RIGHT: *A terrace provides the setting for the wedding reception, with views of the garden beyond providing the backdrop to the celebrations. A colour scheme of blues and pinks against white gives the scene a summery prettiness.*

OPPOSITE, ABOVE LEFT: *Glasses with coloured stems double up as place markers, and fabric roses sit on the hand-decorated plates.*

OPPOSITE, ABOVE RIGHT: *The favours are concealed in pink boxes decorated with sheer ribbon and a fresh pink rosebud.*

Did you know THAT WHITE WEDDINGS WERE POPULARIZED BY THE VICTORIANS? BEFORE THEN, BRIDES WORE THEIR BEST DRESS, SOMETIMES WITH THE ADDITION OF A WHITE RIBBON TO SYMBOLIZE PURITY.

RELAXED WEDDING

Smaller wedding receptions are perfectly suited to more informal surroundings, making guests feel welcome, at ease and at home. This setting is the terrace of a country house, where the scents, sights and sounds of a summer garden can be enjoyed without worrying about bad weather. The emphasis is on colour, with white acting as a foil for candy pink, baby blue and accents of deep pink. Flowers are an important motif for this table setting, since the whole garden and its glorious flowers are the backdrop for the occasion.

A white linen tablecloth covers the table completely. Using a covering which reaches to the floor – whether it be a tablecloth, sheet or length of fabric – produces a clean look, concealing distracting table legs. The napkins are in shades of palest pink and blue rather than the usual white, alternating round the table. Folding metal garden chairs have been smartened up with seat and back covers in a rose- and stripe-patterned fabric that picks out the day's key colours. Chinese-style paper lanterns hold nightlights and hang from a garland

of ivy swagged between the arches of the terrace. Lighting plays an important role in creating an intimate, romantic atmosphere, and outdoor fairy lights, flares stuck in the ground or metal lanterns placed along a wall would all work well, casting a magical glow as the evening approaches.

On the tables, glasses with pastel-coloured stems, to which name tags have been tied with narrow ribbon, continue the colourful theme. The white china has freehand circular patterns drawn into the glaze, and each plate is decorated with a lush fabric cabbage rose. Nightlights are placed inside cream-painted wire baskets, the open sides casting intricate shadows across the table. The favours have been packaged in two ways. Some sit on gilt-edged china, housed in magenta boxes tied with sheer ribbon and finished with a rose. Others, in white boxes with white ribbon, have been arranged on a cake stand that also displays the table number, creating a simple but striking centrepiece.

OPPOSITE, ABOVE LEFT: *Nightlights inside Chinese lanterns provide a romantic glow as day turns into evening.*
OPPOSITE, BELOW LEFT: *More favours, this time arranged on a cake stand as a centrepiece for the table.*
OPPOSITE, RIGHT: *Folding metal garden chairs are dressed up with fabric seat and back covers.*
ABOVE LEFT: *Candles flicker inside cream-painted wire baskets.*
ABOVE RIGHT: *Pale pink and blue napkins are in keeping with the wedding's colourful theme.*

CLASSIC WEDDING

The classic wedding look is one governed by tradition and formality. It is a style that lends itself to grand locations, such as stately homes or country-house hotels. Surroundings as majestic as this – a panelled room with lofty proportions and a spectacular chandelier – must be the starting point for your scheme. Take your cue from your venue's colour scheme, then create a look in sympathy with it. Here, a white, cream and gold theme was suggested by the wall colour and the marble fireplace and gilded mirror. The fireplace dominates the room, forming a natural focal point that lends itself to decoration. The three-armed candelabra have been echoed by a candle still life in the empty grate. Large church candles of different heights form a magical display that creates a sense of welcome and celebration.

This is a rich, lavish scheme but not an overwhelming one, thanks to the exceptionally light and airy quality of the space. Flowers, used in extravagant abundance, play a key role. Roses, tulips, mimosa, snowberries and ivy have

ABOVE LEFT: Large church candles bring a warm, romantic glow to the empty hearth, creating a sense of welcome. Various heights have been used to create the best effect when the candles are lit.
ABOVE RIGHT: Open-backed gilt chairs are a popular choice for weddings. They look particularly pretty with flower arrangements cascading down the back.
OPPOSITE: An imposing marble fireplace and ornate mirror dominate this room, offering a natural focal point and the ideal place for an extravagant floral garland.

been used to fashion a magnificent garland across the fireplace, anchored by two floral clusters. The table arrangements sit in silver stands, while the chairs are decorated with cascades of flowers down their backs. The effect is soft and romantic.

A pristine white tablecloth sets the tone for the sumptuous table setting. The dinner service is white with a gold rim, with one gold-striped plate used to provide visual contrast. Gilt-edged glassware continues the theme. Gold dominates the table, right down to the ribbon adorning the chocolate favours. Contrasting accents of silver – in the form of cutlery and flower stands – have been deliberately introduced to ensure that the effect doesn't become oppressively opulent. In the same way, gilt chairs with open backs have been used in preference to solid chairs. This is a look of great refinement and elegance, extravagant without being fussy, formal without being rigid.

Did you know THAT THE PRACTICE OF HOLDING A WEDDING RECEPTION HAS ITS ROOTS IN THE MEDIEVAL PERIOD? THE GROOM WAS SUPPOSED TO GIVE GIFTS OF FOOD AND DRINK TO HIS IN-LAWS IN ORDER TO DEMONSTRATE THAT HE COULD SUPPORT HIS NEW WIFE.

OPPOSITE AND LEFT: *The gold-and-white dinner service and gold-rimmed glassware have a look of stately elegance. Bags of chocolate truffles, tied with gold ribbon, await the guests.*
FAR LEFT: *The table flowers, arranged in a domed shape, sit in gleaming silver stands.*
ABOVE: *A floral swag decorates the majestic fireplace, held in place by two loose clusters of flowers that echo the table arrangements.*

LEFT: *A posy of flowers tied with green ribbon decorates the back of one of the chairs to mark the head of the table.*
OPPOSITE: *Weeping willows are a glorious backdrop for the pink, green and white tables. Flowers are are the key motif, from the centrepieces to the patterned china and favours.*

ABOVE: *Country flowers such as lupins, roses, stock and blackberries overflow from glass vases on the table.*
BELOW: *The bridesmaids' bouquets, composed of the same flowers, have been tied with a big bow of green satin ribbon.*

COUNTRY WEDDING

A summer garden is a reception setting of enormous charm and romance. You'll need to feel extremely confident of fine weather to risk an entirely alfresco celebration, so having a marquee will probably form part of your plans. A rural location is very much a blank canvas, leaving you free to decide whether you want the reception to be a formal affair or a laid-back occasion, with children and pets running across the lawn. The mood here is relaxed, with the emphasis on cottage-garden flowers and a colour scheme of pink and green, prompted by the verdant surroundings.

For the meal, simple trestle tables have been set end to end and covered with white cotton sheets to cover the legs. Large damask tablecloths have been laid on top of this on the diagonal, to create a diamond shape. Collapsible garden chairs provide the seating, although for an at-home wedding, a mix-and-match collection of garden benches and chairs from the

house would have its own charm. Tall glass vases, overflowing with lush flowers, provide a centrepiece. Roses, lupins, cow parsley, stock and ripening blackberries have been used, all in tones of green and pink. To avoid an overly sugary look, rich pinky-reds have been introduced alongside the pastel shades. To mark the head of the table, a bouquet of flowers, tied with wide, green satin ribbon, has been attached to the chair back.

For the table setting, floral china has been chosen to continue the pink and green theme. As with the chairs, for a small wedding at home an assortment of different floral china could work well. A combination of glassware has been used – pale green glass, etched designs and plainer, clear glasses. The whole table setting has been overlaid with a loose web of tiny, green glass hearts on fine wire. The favours, which also act as name cards, are a particularly pretty detail, consisting of small, white boxes decorated with narrow green ribbon and a fresh rose of the sort used in the table arrangements and bouquets.

ABOVE LEFT: *Accents of deeper pinks give the flower arrangements depth. Sweet-smelling stock ensures the air is filled with summer perfume.*
ABOVE RIGHT: *Sunlight filters through the glasses, creating pools of colour on the white cloth.*

the great outdoors

LEFT AND ABOVE: *Trestle tables covered in white cotton sheets and white garden chairs help to set the tone for the reception, ensuring a relaxed and friendly atmosphere. The finished result is idyllic.*

flowers

FLOWERS AND WEDDINGS ARE A MATCH MADE IN HEAVEN.
NOTHING IS MORE ROMANTIC THAN FRESH FLOWERS,
WHETHER CASCADES OF ROSES OR RICHLY SCENTED LILIES.
SURROUNDING YOURSELF WITH FLOWERS WILL ENCHANT
THE SENSES AND LEAVE YOU WITH FRAGRANT MEMORIES.

BRIDAL FLOWERS

ABOVE: A hydrangea head has been sewn on to braid to create a wrist corsage. The green-tinged flowers and pink and green braid echo the wedding's colour theme.

ABOVE CENTRE: A slender sheaf of calla lilies is secured with a eucharis lily tucked into an organza bow, complementing the modern, clean lines of the bride's dress.

The tradition of the bridal bouquet began many centuries ago with brides carrying posies of aromatic herbs to ward off evil spirits. Today, however, a bridal bouquet is purely decorative, and designed to heighten the beauty of the wedding ensemble.

Traditionally, bouquets were wired, an intricate and time-consuming task that produces a formal look. The current vogue is for hand tying bouquets, a technique that gives a looser, more relaxed result. A slender sheaf of flowers, such as lilies, carried in the crook of the arm, takes the style to its most sleek and modern. The more traditional approach is a fuller, rounder bouquet. Although it's usual for the bride to have a larger bouquet than the bridesmaids, there are no rules, so choose whatever suits your dress and makes you happy.

Collaborating with a professional florist is, for most brides, a new experience. For your first meeting with them, take along your treasure trove of inspirational objects (see Planning, pages 8–13), a picture of your dress and a scrap of its fabric. All this will help your florist to envisage the style of wedding that you are trying to create.

THIS PAGE: *Single-variety bouquets have a simplicity about them that lets the beauty of the flowers shine through. This loose posy of exquisite eucharis lilies looks informal and yet luxurious.*
OPPOSITE, ABOVE RIGHT: *The blooms have such a strong form that only one is needed to make a striking headdress.*

Colour is usually the first thing that brides discuss with their florist. White is the classic wedding choice, pure and elegant. There are few things more exquisite than a flawless bouquet of white roses or lilies. Pink is a feminine, romantic choice, particularly the paler, blushing tones, while it can create a bold effect at the deeper end of the spectrum. Blue flowers are cool and serene, and there are some good candidates if it's your favourite colour: bluebells in spring; cornflowers and delphiniums in summer; and hydrangeas in late summer and early autumn. Purples are dramatic at their darkest and ethereal when they're shades of mauve and lilac. Yellow is cheerful and positive, while orange is richer and fiery. Red is the colour of passion. The brightest reds are a good match for the intense light of a summer day, while cooler reds look wonderful in winter. Green is, of course, the colour of foliage, but there are also green-tinged flowers which can be used to produce a fresh, tranquil look, such as lady's-mantle, guelder rose and cymbidium orchids.

Did you know THAT BOUQUETS BEGAN THEIR LIFE CENTURIES AGO AS POSIES OF AROMATIC HERBS, CARRIED BY THE BRIDE BECAUSE IT WAS THOUGHT THAT THEY HAD THE POWER TO WARD OFF EVIL SPIRITS?

OPPOSITE, ABOVE
LEFT AND BELOW
LEFT: *Hair accessories
for the bridesmaids have
been made by wiring fresh
flowers on to a hairslide
and an Alice band.*
OPPOSITE, BELOW
RIGHT: *The
bridesmaids' flowers are
similar to the bride's
bouquet, but with some
accents of deeper colour
from roses and ripening
blackberries.*
LEFT: *High romance for
high summer: this bouquet
is an unashamedly pretty
mixture of soft pinks and
white, and includes roses,
carnations and scabious.*

THIS PAGE: *Hydrangeas are wonderful for late summer and early autumn colour, and are available in a range of pinks and blues, from very pale through to red and almost purple. The rounded softness of the many-petalled heads helps to create a very feminine, romantic look.*

pink perfection

Single-colour bouquets are always popular, whether using exactly the same shade or a mixture of light and dark tones, but you might want a more eclectic approach. Colours which lie next to each other on the colour wheel – such as yellow and orange, or purple and pink – produce harmonious partnerships. Colours that sit opposite each other, such as blue and orange, or red and green, create more vibrant effects. Using pale shades will tone down a combination, while darker ones will intensify it. If this sounds daunting, remember that it's a professional florist's job to know how to use colour. As a starting point, browse around your local florists, seeing which flowers immediately grab you and how they look together.

You can then think about the flowers you want to use. Many of the best-loved flowers are available all year round, among them roses, tulips, carnations, orchids and lilies. They all come in a wide range of colours and last well as cut flowers, and it's extremely useful for

THIS PAGE: *For this bridesmaid's bouquet, palest pink hydrangeas have been surrounded by their own lush green leaves and secured with pink satin ribbon. The bouquet matches the cake shown opposite (and on page 75).*

florists to have these stalwarts to rely on at any time of year. However, it's worth using seasonal flowers since they'll be easily available and are often good value for money. In spring there are daffodils, tulips, ranunculuses, anemones and bluebells; in summer there are sweet peas, cornflowers, peonies and delphiniums. Autumn flowers include hydrangeas, chrysanthemums, Michaelmas-daisies and many berries; winter offers amaryllis, hellebores, snowdrops, pansies and camellias.

Although the appearance of flowers is all-important, don't forget that many of them smell as wonderful as they look. Although we all associate roses with glorious perfume, many of the varieties bred for the floristry trade are scentless. If it's a heady aroma that you want, let your florist know when you first meet. It may be that you will need to use garden varieties begged from generous family and friends. Other flowers at the top of the scent chart are lily of the valley, gardenias, stephanotis, sweet peas and jasmine.

rich reds

ABOVE LEFT AND RIGHT: *Roses look wonderful used on their own because they create a dense, textured effect when they're tightly packed together. Dark, luscious, velvety red roses are a particularly effective choice for a winter wedding.*

LEFT AND BELOW: *Tulips are excellent value and available all year round in a huge range of colours. Massed together, they make for an exuberant bouquet. Here, the stems have been bound with wide wire-edged ribbon that is fastened in place with pearl-headed dressmaker's pins. Another length of ribbon has been wound round the stems and finished with a large bow.*

Did you know THAT IN THE LANGUAGE OF FLOWERS, ROSES SYMBOLIZE LOVE; LAVENDER, DEVOTION; VIOLETS, FAITHFULNESS; LILIES OF THE VALLEY, SWEETNESS AND PURITY; AND GYPSOPHILA, FRUITFUL MARRIAGE?

There are, of course, other ingredients which can be used in bouquets in combination with flowers. In winter, bare twigs or seed heads can look very striking. Sprays of wired beads add glamorous sparkle to a bouquet, as do feathers or wired sequinned butterflies. You can mist spray paints over flowers (metallics are an obvious choice) and even douse them with glitter (both these techniques work particularly well on roses, which are robust enough to carry off such effects). For a soft, romantic look, envelop your bouquet in a cloud of tulle.

Although the stem of a bouquet serves the very practical purpose of being there for the bride to hold on to, it can be used to decorative effect, too. One way to conceal the stem of a bouquet is to bind it completely with thick ribbon, fixing the ribbon in place with pearl-headed dressmaker's pins. Alternatively, a bouquet can simply be hand-tied. Fashioning the ribbon into a large bow always looks pretty (wire-edged ribbon holds its shape well). You

RIGHT: *Using ribbon to tie or bind a bouquet adds an extra element of colour and decoration. The organza ribbon tying this cluster of white roses links up with other touches of blue used throughout the wedding.*

could also use long lengths of ribbon in various harmonizing shades, and leave the ends trailing like streamers. All these exquisite finishing touches help to heighten the beauty of a bridal bouquet.

The style of your flowers is a natural extension of the rest of the wedding, and you'll probably have set the tone of the day by the time you plan your flowers. If the occasion is going to be chic and modern, you'll want flowers with a striking, architectural quality, such as arum lilies or moth orchids. For a very formal wedding, you may want a structured bouquet with lots of classic white wedding flowers, such as roses, stephanotis and gardenias. For a summer

country wedding, a large, loose bunch of cottage-garden favourites such as sweet peas, lupins and poppies would be perfect. If your wedding is fun and informal, a bouquet of sunflowers might appeal. You'll need to decide if you want a large, dramatic bouquet or something smaller and more compact, and whether you want a floral headdress. For bridesmaids there are lots of possibilities, including (for younger bridesmaids) garlands, decorated hoops, floral balls and flower-filled baskets. Whatever kind of arrangement you choose, it's vital that you feel comfortable carrying it, a consideration that's also important for young bridesmaids, who'll soon tire of cumbersome bouquets.

Flowers are a potent symbol of love and celebration and have played a part in wedding festivities for centuries – the Romans, for instance, sprinkled rose petals on the marriage bed. Whether you choose a magnificent armful of roses or a bunch of cow parsley tied with ribbon, enjoy their fleeting beauty and savour their memory long after the day is over.

country chic

ABOVE AND BELOW RIGHT: *'Tails' of ribbon in shades of blue and white add a pretty touch to these informal, rustic bouquets for bride and bridesmaids. The flowers used include roses, delphiniums and lupins.*
RIGHT: *There's no reason why beloved pets shouldn't look their best on the big day, too.*
OPPOSITE: *A mixed bouquet of white garden flowers, including stock and roses, looks charming, delicate and fresh, with crisp white ribbon binding the stems to continue the single-colour theme.*

OPPOSITE AND THIS PAGE: *At a romantic country wedding, pure white is the predominant colour, with accents of soft blue, pink and green, a palette concocted from roses, stock, freesias and snowberries. Floral headdresses, a ribbon sash decorated with roses, and posies with streaming ribbons, all add to the carefree fête champêtre effect. A decorated wicker wheelbarrow adds a touch of whimsy.*

BUTTONHOLES

It's traditional for the groom's buttonhole, or boutonnière, to take its cue from the bride's bouquet. There's no reason to follow the idea literally, of course, but it does add to the overall coherence of the flower scheme if the buttonholes echo the composition of the bride's and bridesmaids' flowers.

It's usual for the groom, best man, father of the bride and ushers to wear special buttonholes, but there may be other men you'd like to extend the courtesy to, such as brothers or the groom's father. You could even consider providing buttonholes as favours for all your male guests, displayed on trays or in baskets at the entrance to the wedding ceremony venue. If you do this, give one of the ushers the job of handing them out, and make sure you've got a plentiful supply of pins.

A single rose is the classic choice for a buttonhole and there are few things which look as elegant. However, there are plenty of other smart possibilities, from individual flowers to combining several. Try a flawless single tulip, gardenia or camellia, or miniature narcissi, ranunculuses, lilies of the valley, or orchids. Foliage is important, too, and helps to frame the flowers.

Consider scent when choosing flowers for buttonholes, since they are placed at just the right level to be smelled by the wearer. Hyacinth florets,

OPPOSITE, ABOVE:
This yellow and white buttonhole of orchids, white irises and mimosa has had its stem bound with narrow ribbon in an elegant criss-cross pattern.

OPPOSITE, BELOW: *Buttonholes don't have to be uniform in composition. Here, a selection of complementary arrangements is displayed on an ornate tray, ready for collection by male members of the bridal party.*

LEFT: *Unusual combinations can produce charming results. Here, rosebuds and heather (for luck) partner each other, their stems bound in lustrous velvet ribbon.*

Did you know THAT THE TRADITION OF THE GROOM WEARING A FLOWER IN
HIS BUTTONHOLE TAKEN FROM HIS BRIDE'S BOUQUET GOES BACK TO THE MEDIEVAL PERIOD,
WHEN A KNIGHT WORE HIS LADY'S COLOURS AS A LOVE TOKEN?

ABOVE AND ABOVE RIGHT: *Roses make undeniably elegant buttonholes. It's a nice idea for the groom's buttonhole to be distinct from the others. Here, his flawless rose is white, while the other men wear pinky-red blooms.*

stephanotis, roses, sweet peas, jasmine or stock (see picture opposite) would all be wonderfully fragrant. Alternatively, there are aromatic herbs such as rosemary and lavender.

Although a buttonhole is a flower arrangement in miniature, the stem can be wrapped for further decoration in just the same way as a bouquet. Interesting ribbons and braids in seductive colours and textures can be fastened with dressmaker's pins in various ways. Ribbon can be tightly bound around the stem to cover it completely (see page 47); alternatively, it can be wrapped to create a spiral or crossover pattern up the length of the stem. If the ribbon is fine enough, it can be tied into a little bow under the head of the flowers.

ABOVE: *A trio of colourful buttonholes. On the left, summery pink spray roses and rose leaves; in the middle, scented white stock and variegated ivy; on the right, a red rose and dark ivy leaf.*

DECORATIONS
& ARRANGEMENTS

Bouquets are usually a bride's first consideration when planning wedding
flowers. Once chosen, the bouquet will set the style for other flowers at the
wedding, on tables, chairs and around the reception room. The colour scheme
and key flowers usually take their cue from the bridal arrangements, but the
surroundings will also help to determine the look of the reception displays (see
the chapters on Modern, Relaxed, Classic and Country weddings for more
pointers). The level of formality or informality is important. For a traditional,
grand reception, the flowers should have a similar quality. This may take the
form of very precisely placed arrangements, forming a rhythmic display on the

table. Formality may also express itself in the placing of the flowers themselves, as is shown by the artfully angled roses on this page. If the wedding is adopting a more relaxed mood, looser, fuller arrangements with a 'just-picked' quality, spilling over the sides of their containers on to the table tops, may be the answer (see the garden wedding on pages 60–61).

Whatever style you adopt, one vital rule of thumb is to make sure that your table arrangements don't detract from the main business of the day, which is eating, drinking, talking and having fun. Towering displays on table tops will only impede the flow of conversation. Guests should be able to see over or through arrangements easily and be able to reach items on the table such as glasses, salt cellars or butter dishes. Don't forget that beautifully scented flowers on your tables (see page 53) will

OPPOSITE: *An abundance of white and green creates a soft, dreamy look. The centrepieces include calla lilies, alchemilla mollis and guelder rose. A eucharis lily lies on each napkin.*
LEFT AND ABOVE RIGHT: *Single white rosebuds have been stripped of their thorns and lower leaves to striking effect. Displayed in bud vases they are beautifully simple yet romantic.*
ABOVE: *A shallow silver dish crammed with blowsy white roses makes for a luscious, low-level display that guests can easily talk over.*

Did you know THAT IN PAST CENTURIES, PEOPLE
BELIEVED THAT TAKING PIECES OF THE BRIDE'S FLOWERS OR
CLOTHES WOULD HELP THEM SHARE HER GOOD FORTUNE? TO
ESCAPE GRABBING HANDS, THE BRIDE WOULD THROW HER BOUQUET
AS SHE LEFT, THE ORIGIN OF TODAY'S TOSSING THE BOUQUET.

greatly enhance your guests' enjoyment of the reception. If you want something big and spectacular, place these arrangements around the reception room, perhaps standing in corners and alcoves or flanking fireplaces, where they can be appreciated while the meal is eaten.

The containers you use for your arrangements are as crucial to the success of the result as the flowers placed in them. Vases are available in a multitude of materials, sizes and colours, but almost anything can be used to house flowers. Cake stands, bowls, jugs, soup tureens or serving dishes can all be used, or (particularly if you're having a small wedding) you might want to source your own containers from car boot sales or junk shops. There's nothing to say that containers have to match, but if you are going for an eclectic look, strive for one element of continuity – in terms of shape, colour or material – to

OPPOSITE: For this pink- and white-themed wedding, hydrangeas are the key flower. China, cake, napkins and flower arrangements await the guests, laid out on a long table garlanded with ivy and eucharis lilies. A cylindrical vase holds a cluster of frothy hydrangeas, which also form the bridesmaids' bouquets (see page 36) and decorate the cake (see page 75).

LEFT AND ABOVE: The delights of a scented garden have been brought indoors for this reception. Pots of lily of the valley act as favours and place markers, while table numbers are displayed on beribboned pots of jasmine, trained on to wire hoops.

FAR LEFT: A single, perfect bloom is one of the simplest but most beautiful ways to decorate a place setting.

RIGHT: *Chair backs are a good vehicle for extra decoration. This delicate wreath of pompom-like mimosa adds a dash of sunny colour.*

OPPOSITE, ABOVE RIGHT: *A floral ball of roses, tulips and snowberries adds a celebratory touch to a door handle.*

OPPOSITE, BELOW LEFT: *A cluster of soft yellow spray roses sits in a silver pot to finish a gilded place setting.*

OPPOSITE, BELOW RIGHT: *To complement the floral ball shown above, posies of roses, tulips and snowberries adorn the backs of gold chairs and double up as place markers.*

prevent everything looking a jumble. For instance, you could place little clusters of spray roses at every setting in a variety of vintage tea or coffee cups (these could also take the place of favours or double up as place markers). Empty antique scent bottles could be put to similar use. Instead of having one large floral centrepiece per table, you could have lots of small arrangements dotted around the reception (such as the pink roses on pages 56–57) in a mixture of clear glass containers, ranging from cut-glass tumblers to bud vases. If there's an impressive mantelpiece in the room where you're having the reception, why not arrange flowers in a collection of tall, clear glass bottles. If you're using mismatching containers, keep your flowers simple and use a single variety and colour.

Galvanized metal or terracotta pots are ideal for table arrangements, and can be bought at florists or garden centres. They look particularly effective when planted up, although you'll have to do this four to six weeks before the wedding. For a winter wedding, try highly scented paper-white narcissi or, for spring, hyacinths. Alternatives include bedding plants from the garden centre or garden plants (such as the lily of the valley and jasmine on page 53).

glorious gold

THIS PICTURE: *Summer roses and old-fashioned pinks adorn white folding chairs at an outdoor reception.*

RIGHT: *Small posies of fragile pink dog roses have been placed in a collection of antique glassware and dotted around the room as an alternative to large set-piece arrangements.*

THIS PICTURE: *Why not delight your guests' senses to the full at your reception? These fragrant, papery sweet peas, loosely tied with a length of pale pink candy-striped ribbon, will exude their scent throughout the meal.*

Shallow containers are very useful for displaying flower heads, snipped off right at the top of the stem. Since your guests will be able to view them at such close quarters, try something exquisitely formed such as roses, peonies or orchids. Shallow bowls are also perfect for displays of candles and petals floating in water (see pages 128–129). Have one large container in the centre of each table, or place a glass dessert bowl at each place setting containing a single bloom. Large seashells, filled with a drop of water, can be used in the same way. Goldfish bowls look spectacular filled with flower heads and petals, magnifying the blooms and exaggerating their beauty. For an informal country wedding, wicker or wire baskets could be filled with a mass of flowers, or a mixture of flowers and seasonal fruits, for table centrepieces. You could even use humble jam jars, tied round with narrow gingham ribbon and filled with casual bunches of sweet peas or cornflowers.

If you want to make a big statement with your flowers, save any imposing arrangements for a

palest plums and purples

OPPOSITE, ABOVE LEFT: *Roses look particularly effective when tightly packed together to form a domed arrangement.*

OPPOSITE, CENTRE: *Wreaths can be used to decorate walls and doors as well as chairs. Here, variegated ivy is dotted with roses and stephanotis.*

OPPOSITE, BELOW RIGHT: *Table flowers should take their cue from the overall style of the reception. Here, the reception is a formal one and the arrangements reflect this: pink roses and white stephanotis alternate to create a regular effect.*

LEFT: *Make sure that chair-back wreaths – here, a composition of anemones and ivy – are securely attached with ribbon so that they don't slip when guests take their seats.*

Did you know THAT QUEEN VICTORIA'S WHITE SATIN AND HONITON LACE
WEDDING DRESS WAS TRIMMED WITH ORANGE BLOSSOM, TRADITIONALLY ASSOCIATED WITH
FERTILITY BECAUSE THE TREES FLOWER AND BEAR FRUIT AT THE SAME TIME?

OPPOSITE AND THIS PAGE: *An idyllic country garden sets the mood for a relaxed summer wedding. In keeping with the outdoors theme, garden chairs and benches have been used for seating, festooned with garlands of flowers. Garden foliage, roses, feverfew and crab apples add to the rustic look, with arrangements spilling out of galvanized buckets, creating a feeling of informality and abundance.*

position where everyone can appreciate them, perhaps in an alcove or on a pedestal. One approach is to use flowers sparsely, arranging a few tall stems of striking flowers such as orchids, arum lilies or African lilies. For a more romantic look, go for a fuller, softer arrangement such as the blowsy pink hydrangeas on page 52. A more unusual technique is to concentrate guests' eyes on the contents of the container itself. Flower stems can be anchored with smooth pebbles, glass beads or even fruit (pears, apples or slices of citrus fruits can work well). Experiment with filling a cylindrical container with flowers (perhaps bluebells or grape hyacinths) so that their heads sit well down in the container. The glass has the effect of magnifying the flowers, drawing the eyes to them. Another clever technique is to crumple up clear cellophane (available from florists) and stuff it into a cylindrical glass vase. Push flower heads randomly into the cellophane (roses or carnations look good), then slowly fill up with water to produce a 'cracked-ice' effect.

OPPOSITE AND RIGHT: *Posts and pillars are good sites for floral displays, particularly at entrances and exits. Here, the arrangement on the pillar will be the last one the bride and groom see as they leave, and will look good in photographs, too.*

LEFT AND BELOW LEFT: *A pretty wreath attached to the boot of the honeymoon car ensures that the newlyweds will make a stylish departure.*

going away in style

Flower arrangements needn't be limited to tables alone. Chair backs can be used for further decoration and make a welcoming sight for guests. Little posies or paper cones filled with flowers can be attached with a length of ribbon (but do make sure that decorations are firmly attached so that they don't slip when guests sit down). Wreaths look good on chair backs, too, as well as suspended from door and cupboard handles, or fixed to walls, pillars or posts. Floral balls are a pretty idea, and hung from door handles with silky ribbon immediately make an entrance look more inviting and festive. Mantelpieces, benches and long tables all offer an opportunity to employ extravagant floral swags and garlands (see page 60).

Flowers can transform even the humblest of settings, but sadly their beauty is only temporary. Since your floral decorations will have served their purpose by the end of the wedding reception, why not encourage your guests to take them home with them? That way, while you're on honeymoon, guests will be able to continue to enjoy their beauty for several days to come.

confetti

SHOWERING NEWLYWEDS WITH CONFETTI DATES BACK TO
PRE-CHRISTIAN TIMES, WHEN GRAIN WAS THROWN OVER
COUPLES TO ENSURE A FRUITFUL UNION. THIS GESTURE OF
COLLECTIVE HAPPINESS MAY HAVE LOST ITS SYMBOLISM,
BUT IT STILL SUMS UP THE JOYFUL SPIRIT OF THE DAY.

CONFETTI

Confetti has taken many forms over the centuries. While it seems to have started life as grain, the Romans apparently preferred to throw almonds over the happy couple. Centuries later, rice became popular, and is still sometimes used today, but tiny, coloured paper shapes have taken over as the norm.

Paper confetti nowadays comes in every conceivable shape and colour, but in recent years there's been a surge of interest in alternatives. Flower petals, fresh or dried, add a romantic, fairytale air to the proceedings. Roses are one of the best sources and come in a wonderful array of colours, from rich, velvety reds to satiny pinks in every hue and, of course, white. Other possibilities include sweet-smelling lavender, or delphiniums (perfect if blue is your accent colour, since it's relatively rare in the flower kingdom).

Did you know THAT THE WORD 'CONFETTI' IS NINETEENTH-CENTURY IN ORIGIN AND COMES FROM THE ITALIAN WORD FOR BONBON OR SWEET, A REFLECTION OF THE FACT THAT SUGAR-COATED NUTS WERE ONCE THROWN OVER NEWLYWEDS?

If you've got suitable plants in your garden (or a generous friend's), you can pick your own (first thing in the morning, when they're at their freshest). If not, flower petal confetti is available to buy. Try cherry blossom or violas in spring, annuals such as sweet peas in summer, and hydrangeas in later summer and autumn. If you've chosen a vibrant colour scheme, marigolds or gerberas might fit the bill. Birdseed is another possibility and will provide a feast for local

O P P O S I T E : *Paper confetti comes in many shapes and colours, but check with your venue before you throw it.*
O P P O S I T E , I N S E T : *Rosy-red rose petals, gathered from the garden and displayed in a pretty enamelled bowl, beg to be scooped up by the handful.*
L E F T : *These embroidered linen sachets are ideal for confetti and could be given away as favours afterwards.*
A B O V E : *Rice or birdseed confetti is best handed around in little bags or sachets, rather than offered loose.*

THIS PICTURE: *Concoct your own confetti from a mixture of flowers. This pearly-white blend includes hydrangea and rose petals.*
BELOW, INSET: *These embroidered silk bags, stuffed to the brim with velvety rose petals, would be a charming keepsake for the bridesmaids.*

wildlife. All these are biodegradable, a great advantage if your wedding venue does not permit confetti to be thrown (something you should check). The ultimate in no-mess confetti is bubbles, which go down particularly well with children.

You may want to leave it up to your guests to bring confetti, but it adds to the fun if you provide it yourself and give an usher the job of handing it out after the ceremony. Present it loose in baskets or galvanized buckets, or package it up in little cones of decorative paper. If you're having bridesmaids, it's a nice idea to give them all a little fabric bag for confetti, which can be kept afterwards as a memento. What nicer way to start married life than under a shower of silken petals?

THIS PICTURE: *This rustic wire basket is just right for keeping cones of confetti upright. Sheets of handmade paper have been rolled into cones and filled with pink and white fabric petals. A wire-edged ribbon bow decorates the basket's handle.*

cakes

It's extraordinary just what can be conjured up out of simple flour, eggs, butter and sugar. With patience, skill and imagination, a humble cake can be transformed into a work of art and an impressive centrepiece for the reception.

MEMORABLE, MOUTHWATERING CAKES

The wedding cake plays a starring role at a wedding reception. It's usually given a table all of its own, carefully positioned so that guests can admire it as they make their way to their places. The cutting of the cake is a high point in the festivities and one rich in symbolism (cakes have been consumed at weddings since classical times to ensure a fruitful union).

The traditional choice is a three-layered confection, usually embellished with white royal icing. Many cakes still take this as a starting point, though tiers are now often stacked rather than balanced on columns. White has the advantage of being the perfect foil for other colours, whether bright or pale, and a backdrop against which intricate icing shows up well. If you're

OPPOSITE: *The icing on this elegant cake is simple enough for a capable amateur to attempt. Using fashion accessories for decoration – pearl-beaded braid and an organza flower – is an easy and stylish way to heighten the cake's impact.*

RIGHT: *Using fresh flowers – here, roses and aromatic lavender – is another simple but effective way to embellish the clean lines of a simply iced cake.*

going to experiment with colour, do it carefully. Pastels – softest pink, blue or lilac, or cream – are the safest options, while stronger shades are usually best used as splashes or highlights (see the rose-covered cake above). Used subtly, gold, silver or sparkling finishes add glamour (see the glittering butterfly on page 76). If you choose a cake that's dark chocolate (see right), you may want to lighten the effect with splashes of colour. Reds, blues and pinks have been used here, but these could be replaced with creams, apricots and burnt oranges.

As for what lies beneath the icing, a rich fruit mixture is the time-honoured favourite, but it could be plain Madeira, chocolate sponge, coffee, lemon or carrot cake. Having one large cake makes a strong statement, and although you could have a single

RIGHT: *Everyone loves chocolate cake, but all that luscious darkness can look unbridal. Here, a cone-shaped cake, covered in luscious chocolate frills, has been studded with vivid anemones for added contrast and colour.*

Did you know THAT THE TRADITIONAL MULTI-TIERED WEDDING CAKE IS BASED ON THE SHAPE OF THE SPIRE AT St BRIDE'S CHURCH IN LONDON?

layer, a stacked or tiered version makes it easier to appreciate the decoration. As an alternative, an arrangement of gorgeously decorated cupcakes, one for each guest, on a series of cake stands would look stunning (see page 70). You could play around with different-coloured icing and toppings of real or sugar flowers, iced hearts or initials, or sweets. These could double up as favours and be presented to guests as they leave.

Icing and sugar paste are amazingly versatile materials and, in the hands of an expert, can be turned into virtually anything, from flowers that look like the real thing to intricate patterns as fine as lace. Your source of inspiration may

THIS PAGE AND ABOVE LEFT:
A delicate posy of pink hydrangeas sits on each layer of this tiered cake. The lacy effect of the blooms harmonizes with the icing pearls defining the base of each tier.

THIS PAGE AND OPPOSITE, ABOVE LEFT: *This spectacular white chocolate cake looks irresistibly creamy and rich. The dainty embellishments add contrasting texture and movement – quivering paper butterflies on the lower tiers and a glinting, sequinned butterfly on top, nestling upon ruffled chocolate and a white-and-gold-striped ribbon.*

be your shared interests or something that recalls the way you met. Another approach is to echo the wedding dress itself, and mimic beading, fabric or embroidery in icing. If icing doesn't appeal, decorative alternatives include fresh fruit (perhaps frosted with sugar) and sugared almonds or other sweets. Of course, decorations needn't be edible. Fresh flowers always look pretty (though make absolutely sure that they haven't been sprayed with chemicals), as do velvety rose petals, fabric flowers, braid, ribbon and other trimmings.

Finally, don't forget the table on which the cake sits. Like a picture frame, it must show off the beautiful creation it bears. Consider using a special tablecloth, posies of flowers, or a scattering of petals or sugared almonds, and place the cake knife, tied perhaps with a beautiful ribbon, alongside two champagne flutes to anticipate the happy toasts to come.

natural abundance

A B O V E : *This very feminine square stacked cake has been covered in basketweave icing. The blowsy roses in palest pastel shades that spill over each layer enhance the cake's demure, ladylike 1950s charm.*

table settings

GUESTS SPEND MUCH OF THE RECEPTION SEATED, SO THE
WAY TABLES ARE DECORATED CAN DO MUCH TO SET THE
MOOD AND ENCOURAGE A CONVIVIAL ATMOSPHERE. USE
CHINA, GLASSWARE, FLOWERS AND LINENS CREATIVELY TO
MAKE YOUR TABLES A PLEASURE TO FEAST AT.

BELOW: *These garden tables have been covered with dainty, old-fashioned, hand-embroidered tablecloths. The favours (in the background) have been tied with a variety of colourful ribbons, to pick up the colours used in the embroidery.*

CHINA, GLASS & SILVERWARE

A wedding reception is your opportunity to welcome and entertain your guests. It's a thank you to everyone for coming and a group celebration of a joyous occasion. Taking the time and trouble to plan attractive table settings shows how much you value your guests. The pleasure that they'll feel at seeing a beautifully laid-out table when they take their seats will do much to create a special, celebratory atmosphere. Unlike large floral displays in a church or civil ceremony venue, which are designed to be seen from a distance, a table setting is viewed in close-up, so small details won't go unnoticed. One way to give your tables a distinctive look is to use objects in unusual ways: tumblers or shot glasses for tiny posies; wine goblets or glass dessert bowls for floating single blooms in; floral teacups or cake stands for displaying favours.

Colour is a good place to start when planning your table settings. Your scheme should complement the bridal flowers and dress to give the day a coordinated look. An all-white scheme is easy to put together and will work best if there are plenty of different textures – embossed china, heavy damask table linen, diaphanous ribbon napkin rings, fresh roses and so on. For an even less colourful, almost ethereal look, you could focus on transparency, with glass or Perspex taking

OPPOSITE, ABOVE, AND THIS PAGE: *This romantic table setting features antique floral plates combined with plain white china. The pattern on the plates inspired a wedding colour scheme of gold, blue and pink, which is repeated in the flowers, liqueur glasses and ribbon-tied roses that lie upon each plate.*

THIS PAGE: *Pistachio green, palest pink and white is the scheme that unites this table setting. The scalloped plates are complemented by the napkins, which have been tied with floral braid. The white tablecloth has been overlaid with embroidered muslin bearing the same motif.*

OPPOSITE, ABOVE: *A wire garland of green glass hearts has been laid across each plate at this setting – a romantic touch that enhances the green detail on the china.*

a starring role (see pages 90–91). Even with a white scheme, however, introducing interest in the form of touches of colour such as green, silver or gold is very effective (see pages 84 and 87). Pastel colours work well together and, of course, with white. Using rich, dark colours is a bold choice and can look magnificent (see page 88), but it needs to be done with restraint.

Whatever your featured colours, the backdrop to a table setting is always the table itself, or rather what goes on top of it – the table linen. Tablecloths and napkins can be cotton, linen or a man-made mixture and come in a variety of weaves or finishes, the classic choice being damask. Table linen can be hired in a rainbow of colours as well as whites, ivories and creams. A neutral backdrop is the easiest to work with, but coloured napkins can look very pretty, particularly if one or two pastel shades are contrasted with a white cloth. Napkins themselves are astonishingly versatile and can be dressed up in all manner of ways to turn them into decorative features in their own right (see pages 92–99). For extra interest on the table, cloths can be

feminine florals...

RIGHT: *This Perspex-handled cutlery is a departure from the norm and would look good with any white table setting.*
FAR RIGHT: *A colour scheme may be prompted by the finest detail. Here, it's the blue border of this Italian china.*

THIS PAGE: *An engraved glass pear makes an exquisite focal point. The pear is decorated with an organza ribbon scattered with gold stars, which accentuates the gilt border on the plates.*
OPPOSITE, ABOVE LEFT: *A silver cake knife is dressed up with a large, floppy bow.*

BELOW: *If you have access to just a few pieces of beautiful family silverware, such as this embossed knife and fork, why not use them for the place settings on the top table?*

layered, with the top ones being laid diagonally to create a diamond pattern. Alternatively, runners can be placed over tablecloths to add texture, pattern and colour. Sheer fabrics, patterned or embroidered (see page 82), are pretty, or experiment with organza or shot silk for a glamorous effect.

Most receptions involve a meal, and the china it is served on should show off the food as well as create a decorative effect. Much of the china available to hire is plain white or has a fine gold or silver rim, styles that are effective foils for any colour scheme. Hunting down decorative tableware may be more difficult, although good catering companies or party planners often have access to less run-of-the-mill designs. If your wedding is a small one, you may be able to take advantage of your own or your family's china collections. Mixing and matching china in

Did you know THAT TRADITIONALLY THE MOST POPULAR TIME OF THE YEAR TO MARRY WAS BETWEEN SEPTEMBER AND CHRISTMAS, WHEN FOOD WAS AT ITS MOST PLENTIFUL?

OPPOSITE: *A gleaming silver pot is an elegant and gracious way to serve coffee. Petits fours, arranged on an antique silver cake stand, are a pretty and moreish accompaniment.*

THIS PICTURE AND INSET: *Patterned glasses add interest to the table. For this sophisticated table setting, silver-edged china determines the theme. Sheer metallic ribbon and modern cutlery finish the look.*

RIGHT: *Using deep, rich colours against a white backdrop makes a strong statement that does not become overpowering. Pinky-red flowers, china, glassware and candles give this table setting a grand, dramatic character that is still pretty and feminine.*

OPPOSITE, LEFT: *Distinctive glassware makes a subtle but unmistakable decorative contribution to the table.*

OPPOSITE, RIGHT: *A pink-rimmed, antique glass dish holds a tempting array of sugared almonds, bringing height and pretty pastel tones to the table.*

what is called a harlequin setting can look very charming and would suit an informal style of reception. Another effective way of using china is to combine plain white with a patterned charger (a large underplate on which the rest of the setting is placed). If the only china available to you is plain and you want a more decorative effect, make full use of napkins and napkin rings, ribbons or fresh flowers, placed on top of the plates. Don't limit yourself to plates and bowls when you're choosing tableware. You can use candlesticks; decorative dishes, bowls and cake stands; pretty cups for coffee; even elaborate condiment sets.

Glassware adds welcome height to a table setting and often colour and pattern, too. Glass can be etched, embossed or engraved for subtle or ornate effects, and styles with tinted stems or bowls can be useful for reinforcing colour schemes. Wineglass or champagne flute stems are good places for adding decoration – ribbon, beads or flowers – and securing name

Did you know THAT FOR TOASTS, THE GLASS SHOULD BE RAISED IN THE RIGHT HAND AND HELD OUT STRAIGHT FROM THE SHOULDER? THIS MEDIEVAL PRACTICE DEMONSTRATED THAT THE TOASTER WAS NOT CONCEALING WEAPONS IN HIS CLOTHING, PROVING THAT HE CAME IN FRIENDSHIP.

tags. They can even be used for placing favours in (see pages 112 and 122). You may want to use glass vases for your table flowers; if you do, make sure they're not so tall or large that they'll prevent eye contact between guests across the table.

Cutlery is often given little thought, but the style you choose needs to complement the rest of the setting, particularly if you're going for a minimalist look, which will demand something equally sleek and simple. Most hire companies provide cutlery of traditional design, which complements most table settings with an element of formality. If you have access to family silver but not in sufficient quantity to set at every place, reserve it for the top table or the bride and groom's places to mark them out as special. The cake knife plays an important symbolic role at the reception (using it is supposed to be the newlyweds' first joint act together), so you might want to dress it up with a bow (see page 85).

Attractive presentation of your reception tables will greatly enhance everyone's enjoyment of the day, enabling your guests to feast their eyes while they fill their stomachs. Even if the elements at your disposal are plain and simple, clever embellishment with napkins, flowers and favours will take them out of the ordinary and turn them into something memorable.

crystal clear

ABOVE: *A napkin has been made into a
fan (fold in half, then half again, then nip
in one corner with ribbon) and decorated
with tiny crab apples, for which any small
fruits (kumquats or physalis, perhaps) or
flowers could be substituted.*

NAPKINS

Although napkins serve a straightforwardly practical purpose (particularly on a day when everyone is dressed in their finery), they can be turned into a highly decorative part of the table setting.

In the seventeenth century, it became the practice to use large white napkins on formal occasions such as weddings. A starched white or cream napkin in damask or plain-weave linen, as generously proportioned as possible, remains the classic choice. Linen double damask is considered the finest quality since it is self-patterned on both sides of the fabric. Although white is the obvious wedding colour for table linen, providing an ideal backdrop for the table setting, using coloured napkins is a way of personalizing the tablescape. Pastels, such as candy pink, baby blue or pistachio green, look romantic and summery and could work well if they pick up on an accent colour used for the wedding dress or flowers. For an autumnal wedding, you might

OPPOSITE, ABOVE RIGHT: *Lengths of
ready-made ruffled white ribbon have been joined
to make these feminine napkin rings.*
THIS PAGE: *Scour haberdashery departments
and craft shops for interesting braids, buttons,
trims and ribbons, which can be transformed into
unique decorative napkin rings.*

golden wedding

ABOVE: *Cream napkins, embellished with slender gilt hoops, sit on a burnished plate.*
ABOVE RIGHT: *A special napkin ring would make a lovely present for a bridesmaid or mother on the big day. This beautiful, delicate napkin ring looks like a piece of precious jewellery.*

want all the table linen to reflect the rich, warm colours of the season. In summer, the intensity of the light means that it's easier to get away with vibrant brights. Your napkins don't have to match your tablecloth and you might want to use them to introduce an element of pattern or contrasting colour. Whatever colours or patterns you choose, think about how they will work with the food you are serving. One should complement the other.

The classic way to present napkins is to fold them into a rectangle and to rest them on plates so that they just overlap the top and bottom. Whether the napkins lie in the middle of the place setting or to one side is up to you. There are more elaborate approaches to napkin folding. In the seventeenth century there was a fashion for creating extraordinary shapes – animals, birds, butterflies – and professional napkin folders would work their magic in wealthy households in preparation for grand banquets. While such things are beyond most of us, it's easy to fold napkins into pockets (see page 99) so that place

BELOW: *An extravagant beaded tassel brings instant glamour.*
RIGHT: *A pewter bowl holds napkins, each rolled up inside silver fretwork rings with name tags attached.*
BELOW RIGHT: *Classic white china with a silver border is coordinated with napkins tied with shimmering silver ribbon.*

THIS PAGE: *Elegant silk tassels adorned with softest mink pompoms (designed, in fact, as keyrings) make the ultimate in luxurious — and sensual — napkin rings.*

cards, flowers, breadsticks or other decorations can be popped in. Another easy arrangement is to fold napkins into triangles and then roll them up, which also creates a pocket. Napkins can be cinched in the middle (see page 99), or turned into little fans (see page 92), though the easiest way to display them is simply to roll them up and secure them with a ring. If you want your napkins elaborately folded by your caterers, they will have to be well starched to hold their shape.

Decorating napkins opens up a world of possibilities, from the elaborate to the simple. Lots of the best effects can be achieved with everyday materials and minimal effort. Napkins that have been folded into rectangles and placed on plates can be embellished with single flowers to romantic effect. Fresh herbs such as lavender or rosemary can be used, or perhaps homemade biscuits, cut into hearts. Fruits also look effective, as do daisy chains, rose petals and sugared almonds.

One of the easiest and prettiest ways to secure your napkins is to roll them up and tie decorative ribbon around them. Wide ribbon can be turned into napkin rings, as can lace, braid, cord or other

ABOVE LEFT: *Roses and weddings go hand in hand. This white porcelain rose and the napkin it encircles create a look of pure, timeless elegance.* LEFT: *Upholstery braid has been used here as a napkin ring. The pretty flower motif picks up a theme of pistachio green, pink and white, which is repeated throughout the table setting.*

delicate details

ABOVE: *A neat row of embroidered napkins awaits the cutting of the cake, with pastry forks slipped beneath napkin rings of pink ribbon.* ABOVE RIGHT: *Three variations on a white-on-white theme: a shell threaded on to ribbon; a button on ribbon; and a satin-bound pipe cleaner clasping a single perfect pearl.*

trims (see page 93). Wire-edged ribbon is particularly good as it holds its shape so well. Keep a lookout in haberdashery departments or craft shops for interesting materials. Beads could be threaded on to wire, ribbon or yarn to make napkin rings. Consider using shells, pearly buttons and tassels in the same way. Junk shops can also yield surprising finds, such as old crystal chandeliers, whose droplets can be threaded and tied around napkins, or vintage costume jewellery. Homemade biscuits can be threaded on to ribbon (pierce holes in them before baking). Your napkins could also be encircled by stems of ivy or blades of long, strong grass such as bear grass (available from your florist), or chives.

Even with something as commonplace and utilitarian as napkins there's lots of fun to be had by turning them into a decorative feature on the table. Your guests will then have the pleasurable job of unfolding them in preparation for the feasting that's to follow.

THIS PAGE: *Folding napkins can create pretty effects. The left-hand napkin was folded in half, then into three and tied at the top with ribbon. The middle one has been folded diagonally and cinched with a fabric rose. On the right, the napkin has been made into a pouch, with a place card slipped in.*

Claudia

PLACE CARDS & TABLE NUMBERS

Drawing up a seating plan for the reception can be one of the most taxing and time-consuming parts of pre-wedding planning. Trying to choreograph things so that old friends will have a chance to catch up, new friendships will be forged and relatives won't feel left out can tie everyone in knots. However, it's the best way to avoid an unseemly scramble for places and disappointed guests. Once the hard work is out of the way, reward yourself by having fun displaying your place cards and table numbers. Even though they're a small detail, they're an important one, helping to set the tone for the feast to come and ensure that everyone knows where they're going.

If you've got attractive handwriting, you could pen the cards yourself. It's worth getting hold of a proper fountain pen for the purpose, or buying a calligraphy kit. Black ink will read most clearly, but you could choose sepia for a soft, romantic look, or brightly coloured inks, perhaps using one colour for male guests and another for female. Stationers and art shops sell metallic pens, though these inks are sometimes less visible from a distance.

The classic hands for formal stationery are italic, the elegant script developed in the Vatican at the end of the fifteenth century; and copperplate, a

Did you know THAT THE ORIGIN OF THE TERM 'HONEYMOON' IS THE OLD PRACTICE OF NEWLYWEDS DRINKING MEAD — SYMBOLIC OF LIFE AND FERTILITY, AND MADE FROM FERMENTED HONEY — FOR A MONTH AFTER THEIR WEDDING?

OPPOSITE: *This ivy wreath is decked with paper leaves, held in place with gilt butterflies, on which names and table numbers are written in gold.*

ABOVE RIGHT: *A name tag, decorated with a little white rose (like those available in haberdashery departments), is tied to the lid of a soup cup.*

BELOW LEFT: *The slender stem of a wineglass is an obvious place to tie a name tag. Secure them with wire, ribbon or braid.*

BELOW RIGHT: *You may be lucky enough to have decorative objects with which to dress your tables. Here, an exquisite porcelain pagoda holds a nightlight and acts as a table marker.*

Teaspoons with colourful enamel handles, set atop neat rows of coffee cups and saucers, have been tied with matching velvet ribbon and tags to act as both favours and place cards.

ABOVE RIGHT AND OPPOSITE: *This table number was fashioned from florist's wire then threaded with blue beads. It is encircled by handmade biscuits, iced with guests' names and indicating their places. The gorgeous pastels create a feminine, romantic look.*

fine hand based on that used in copperplate engravings from the seventeenth century onwards. A computer is a quicker option, and has the advantage of being easier to correct mistakes on. Most programs seem to have a huge array of fonts, from the classic to the wacky. The other option is to have the place cards printed along with the wedding invitations, or commission a professional calligrapher. Whichever method you choose, make sure the hand is easy to decipher, even from a distance. If your wedding is small and intimate, you may be able to get away with using first names alone for the place cards, but with a larger gathering write the guests' names in full. Don't forget to put someone in charge of a master copy of the seating plan, just in case any cards get dropped or otherwise mislaid.

The usual material for place cards is white or cream card, but you could alternatively use a pastel colour, particularly if it ties in with detail on the wedding dress or the bouquets. Another possibility is heavy or textured paper.

teatime treats

THIS PAGE: *For this immaculate white-on-white setting, napkins have been tied in the middle with gold ribbon and draped over the plates. The place cards sit above and just to the left of each plate, held in silver card holders.*

You could even write the names (preferably in white or a metallic) on thick, glossy leaves, such as laurel. To give place cards an individual touch, experiment with patterned craft scissors or pinking shears to produce a decorative edge.

You'll need not only to put a card at each place setting but also to display a seating plan. The simplest way to do this is to print it out on a piece of paper, grouping guests' names under each lettered or numbered table. However, it adds to the fun to approach it a bit more creatively. The formal custom is to have small envelopes bearing the name of each guest, with the table number written on a card inside. For a more relaxed feel, you could have folded or tented cards with both the name and table number on them. Set out the cards on a large table so that more than one person at a time can collect them, somewhere near the entrance to the reception. It looks very elegant to lay the cards out in neat rows, perhaps along lengths of wide ribbon that have been pinned to the tablecloth. You could ask your florist to make you a floral 'cushion' for them to rest on by inserting flowers, their stems

ABOVE LEFT: *This simple idea gains its impact by being executed on a grand scale. Champagne flutes, arranged in ordered rows, each hold a single flower, to whose stem a name tag has been tied.*
ABOVE RIGHT: *This pearl-beaded number '2' was shaped from wire and nestles in a bed of sugared almonds to make a delectable centrepiece.*

ABOVE: *White and silver combine to make a subtle colour scheme. The napkins are nipped in with wire, with a heart-shaped shell ornament and name tag attached.*
ABOVE CENTRE: *You may want to invest in special place-card holders for the top table as mementoes of the day. This delightful porcelain bunny would undoubtedly become a treasured keepsake.*
ABOVE RIGHT: *Table-top easels can be bought from art shops and are just the right size for holding table numbers. Here, the numbers have been written in gold to echo the gold border on the china.*

simple pleasures

snipped very short, into a block of florist's foam. You could turn place cards into little flags, attach them to cocktail sticks and stick them into individual chocolates or cupcakes, or attach them to small boxes of sweets, wrapped with ribbon. In this way, place cards can double up as favours for guests to take home with them. There's no reason why you shouldn't display place cards on a wall, as the elegant wreath on page 100 shows.

Exercise your inventiveness at place settings, too. Place cards can be attached to little boxes of favours, or to the stems of wineglasses. They could sit in pretty coffee cups; be tucked into napkins or between the layers of pine cones (perhaps sprayed gold or silver); be tied to sprigs of lavender or the stems of roses; or attached to pieces of cutlery with decorative ribbon. Place-card holders can be bought from many stationery or gift shops and can double up as favours to be taken home by the guests.

Table numbers must be a good size and clearly displayed, and they could form part of a larger centrepiece. Whether you use letters of the alphabet or numbers is up to you, but be sure that you stick to one system – numbers on the seating plan and letters on the tables could cause a traffic jam. For a country wedding, you could draw numbers in chalk on little slates, or make jaunty paper flags, glued to kebab skewers, and stick them into jam jars filled with sand and shells. For a more sophisticated approach, numbers could be made by threading beads on to wire. A skilled baker could fashion numbers out of bread or pretzel dough, while an accomplished cake maker could even create them out of pulled sugar.

Although place cards and table numbers are some of the finer points of reception detail, they're fun to exercise your inventiveness on and they help, in however small a way, to make the day a memorable one.

ABOVE AND BELOW LEFT: *Flowers in miniature pots make charming place-card holders, adding height, colour and, in some cases, scent to the table. Try small bulbs, such as grape hyacinths or dwarf narcissi, or garden plants, such as lily of the valley, violas or primulas.*

OPPOSITE AND LEFT: *This spectacular green-on-green centrepiece uses glass balls (try Christmas decorations), on which the table number has been written in thick silver pen, and bunches of grapes on the vine, all piled on to a crystal dish.*

favours

PRESENTING GUESTS WITH A PARTING GIFT AS A MEMENTO
OF THE DAY IS AN AGE-OLD TRADITION. WHETHER IT'S
A BAG OF HOMEMADE BISCUITS OR SOMETHING MORE
PERMANENT, A THOUGHTFUL PRESENT WILL BE SURE TO
BRING A SMILE TO EVERYONE'S FACE.

ABOVE: *Silk flowers and floral ribbon make these favour boxes a gift in themselves.*
ABOVE CENTRE: *A cheerful assortment of ribbons adds to the festive effect of favours piled on a dish.*
ABOVE RIGHT: *Placing this beribboned favour in a glass that echoes the blue of the ribbon heightens its visual impact.*

MEMENTOES & KEEPSAKES

Favours – little gifts for guests to take home with them – have enjoyed a huge rise in popularity in recent years. However, there's nothing new about the concept, which has its roots in classical civilization. In ancient Rome, guests broke bread over the heads of the bride and groom before picking up pieces and eating them, a practice which centuries later evolved into the tradition of having a wedding cake. Taking home a slice of this cake and taking home a favour have the same symbolic meaning – they are a token shared between the newlyweds and their family and friends, reflecting the guests' role in witnessing and supporting the marriage. In time, favours evolved into a gift of five sugared almonds (*bomboniere*, as the Italians call them) to represent health, wealth, long life, happiness and fertility. Almonds have had a long association with weddings due to their link with fruitfulness and abundance. There is also the idea that a bitter almond with a sweet coating reflects the wedding vow 'for better or for worse'. Nowadays, favours can be any small gift, distributed as a thank you to guests for their attendance and to remind them of the wedding.

THIS PAGE: *Tiny, hand-painted enamelled boxes, tied with pastel ribbons, make exquisite, extravagant keepsakes that can be personalized with the date of the wedding or initials of the guests on the base.*

All this symbolism aside, wedding favours are great fun to plan, and are a detail that will charm and surprise your guests. They needn't be fancy or expensive; merely thoughtfully chosen. You could give out little bundles of slender candles, bound with wide ribbon, tiny lanterns (finished with a ribbon bow) or boxes of scented nightlights. Little sachets of potpourri or dried lavender are another sweet-smelling idea. For a gift which will delight guests months after the wedding, wrap up packets of seeds (easy-to-grow annuals, such as sweet peas or larkspur, for instance) or place bulbs in cardboard boxes (including planting instructions). Embroidered handkerchiefs, scented soaps or miniature books are other good possibilities. If your wedding has a strong seasonal slant, select the favours accordingly: perhaps painted or dyed eggs in spring; paper fans for summer; apple- or pear-shaped candles in autumn; and bundles of mulled wine spices, snow shakers or Christmas baubles in winter. Small terracotta or galvanized metal pots, planted up with bulbs or bedding plants, make charming favours and, like many of the other ideas here, can double up as place markers.

OPPOSITE AND THIS PAGE: *Enveloping a favour in a lacy or embroidered handkerchief, which can be personalized with the bride and groom's or guest's initials, means that the lovely wrapping becomes part of the gift. Add a ribbon bow or a dainty fabric rose as a finishing touch.*

pretty parcels

Once you've chosen your favours, you can decide how you'd like to package them. Little envelopes are useful for loose items such as seeds. Seal them with sealing wax for a traditional look, or tie with pretty ribbon, then lay them in neat rows for guests to collect. Small cardboard boxes are easy to decorate and look very enticing when placed at place settings, piled on to serving dishes or laid out neatly on trays or tables. Ribbons are a simple, inexpensive and versatile form of decoration for favour boxes. Either choose one colour of ribbon that links up with the rest of your colour scheme, or use one colour for male guests' favours and another for female, or go for a cheerful assortment of designs (see page 112). Boxes can be adorned with all sorts of trims and braids. Real, paper or fabric flowers look lavishly romantic, while sparkling beads, feathers and sequins provide a glamorous finish. You could also experiment with many different ways of wrapping your boxes, using layers of paper or tissue, bows and ribbon (see page 120).

How and when you give out your favours is a matter of personal taste. If you want favours to be a parting gift, station ushers or staff at the exits to the reception with trays of goodies, or arrange them on a large table. You could display your favours formally, laid out in neat rows, perhaps along runners of

ABOVE: Your favours should continue the wedding colour scheme. Here, pink and green are key colours, picked up by the fresh roses and ribbon embellishing the favours. Sparkling beads are a final, lavish touch
ABOVE RIGHT: Attendants clutch their favours, tied with pastel ribbons, undoubtedly eager to see what's inside.
OPPOSITE: Arranged en masse, these favour boxes, topped with a fabric rose and pink ribbon, look beguilingly pretty.

THIS PICTURE: *This gilded table setting demands equally glamorous favours. Gold boxes finished with an oversized white satin bow look just the part.*

RIGHT: *A diaphanous silk and organza flower sitting in a translucent onyx dish acts as both favour and table decoration.*

THIS PICTURE: *Another extravagant variation on the golden theme: this time a flourish of wire-edged polka-dot ribbon tops the favour box, and is finished with a fabric flower.*

LEFT: *White baby pumpkins, sporting tiny organza bows and piled into a glass serving dish, make an unusual centrepiece and whimsical favours.*
BELOW: *Different widths and shades of metallic ribbon make this favour box look sleek, smart and modern.*

wide ribbon, pinned to a tablecloth, or on top of a scattering of rose petals. For a more informal look, they could be piled into large, shallow bowls or baskets, or stacked on cake stands, with flowers tucked in between the favours for extra decoration. With the addition of name tags, favours also work well as place markers and add a decorative touch to the table when placed on top of each plate. This is a particularly good approach if you're providing something with which guests can amuse themselves during the meal, such as bottles of bubbles. You could also pop in a specially created party game for everyone to try over coffee, such as coming up with anagrams of the bride and groom's names. To emphasize the idea of favours as a thank you, you could ask your bridesmaids to circulate during the reception bearing baskets of treats, handing them out table by table.

A wedding is a hugely enjoyable occasion for guests and also one at which they express their fondness for the bride and groom through the giving of gifts. Favours are a way of making this reciprocal. Whether yours are large or small, simple or extravagant, they'll delight and surprise all who receive them.

Did you know
THAT THE TRADITIONAL CHOICE FOR FAVOURS IS SUGARED ALMONDS, PARTICULARLY IN ITALY, WHERE THEY'RE CALLED BOMBONIERE? FIVE ALMONDS ARE GIVEN TO EACH GUEST, REPRESENTING HEALTH, WEALTH, FERTILITY, HAPPINESS AND LONG LIFE.

EDIBLE FAVOURS

Sugared almonds are the traditional way to tempt wedding guests. Almonds have been a delicacy since ancient times – the Greeks and Romans turned them into sweetmeats by coating them in honey. They're a good choice because they last well and look decorative, coming in a rainbow of colours from pastels to metallics. They're very attractive scattered on tables like confetti or piled into little shallow dishes.

However, anything sweet can be turned into favours, from kitsch but cute love hearts to sophisticated chocolates (if you choose the latter for a summer wedding, keep them cool until the last minute so that there's no risk of melting). Biscuits are appealing, particularly if they are handmade or personalized with guests' initials in pale pink or blue icing. Wedding-cake-shaped biscuits, iced to mimic the real thing, will prompt admiring comments from their recipients. Many professional cake makers now make miniature wedding cakes as favours, which look spectacular presented on each plate. Alternatively, you could package up slices of the real wedding cake in boxes and hand them to guests as they leave (see page 121).

FAR LEFT: *Mouthwatering pink truffles are presented in a china soup bowl, packaged in cellophane and tied with striped gold and white ribbon.*
LEFT: *Bags of sweets, tied with satin ribbon and placed in china cups to mark the end of the meal, make a pretty composition of pink and white.*
ABOVE: *What could be more symbolic of marriage than two gold-wrapped chocolate hearts in a champagne glass?*

THIS PAGE: *A dish of delights: sweets are a good-value choice for favours if you're on a tight budget, and can easily be dressed up with ribbons, bags and boxes to create tempting little treats.*

THIS PAGE: *Handmade, chocolate-covered rose creams, packaged in an illustrated box, have an old-fashioned charm that is emphasized by placing them on a lace doily.*

Did you know THAT IN VICTORIAN TIMES, IT WAS BELIEVED THAT IF AN UNMARRIED FEMALE GUEST SLEPT WITH WEDDING CAKE BENEATH HER PILLOW, SHE WOULD DREAM OF HER FUTURE HUSBAND?

Traditional treats such as clotted-cream fudge or shortbread are always well received, or you could go all-out for fun with multicoloured jelly beans or huge, transparent lollipops, stuck in among a bowl of flowers and placed in the middle of each table. Sweets and biscuits are simple to package prettily. Arrange them in little tissue-paper-lined boxes or place them in the middle of circles of cellophane, net or organza and gather up the edges, tying with ribbon and finishing with a real or fabric flower. Wedding companies sell fabric bags and little aluminium tins, ideal for a handful of mints or gilded chocolate buttons. Although favours are usually something guests take home with them, you might want to offer edible goodies with coffee and have the pleasure of seeing your guests indulging their sweet tooth.

ABOVE LEFT: *Assorted sweets, wrapped in twisted tissue paper in jewelled shades, fill pretty antique coffee cups to the brim.*
ABOVE: *Carefully parcelled in pink paper and topped with tiny paper roses, this Italian marzipan cake looks almost too good to eat.*

candles

IT'S IMPOSSIBLE NOT TO BE MESMERIZED AND FASCINATED BY DANCING FLAMES. CANDLES ARE AN INDISPENSABLE AND VERSATILE TOOL IN THE DECORATOR'S REPERTOIRE, LOOKING GOOD WHATEVER THE STYLE OF WEDDING AND BATHING EVERYTHING IN A WARM, WELCOMING GLOW.

CANDLES

What are weddings about if they are not about romance, and what is more romantic than flickering candlelight? Candles bring with them echoes of previous ages, of magic and otherworldliness, as well as religious symbolism and associations with innocence, purity, hope and truth. On a purely aesthetic level, candlelight is softer and more yellow than daylight and is highly flattering, bathing its surroundings in a reassuring, welcoming glow. For all these reasons and more, candles are a beautiful addition to any wedding reception.

If you want to use candles, you must consider safety, particularly as there will be veils and children about, so discuss your plans with staff at the reception venue or marquee company. Moreover, if you're using candles in quantity, you'll need a way to light them all quickly (professionals often use butane torches). Another consideration is how long you want the candles to burn for. Beeswax candles burn more slowly than paraffin-based ones, and are more expensive as a result. However, you should get three or four hours of illumination even from nightlights.

ABOVE LEFT: *Pink floating candles and petals and red roses make a colourful centrepiece.*
ABOVE: *Frosted-glass votives holding scented candles sit on a paper-doily-covered tray.*
BELOW: *A crystal cup, decorated with two lovebirds, holds a candle for the bride and groom.*

THIS PAGE: *Nightlights in dainty glass holders are clustered on a circular mirror that reflects and intensifies their twinkling light.*
INSET: *Pure white candles and eucharis lily heads float serenely in a porcelain bowl.*

THIS PAGE: *A mantelpiece holds a collection of different candles and vintage holders, some decorated with glass beads, along with a lacy puff of white hydrangea for a sparkling, magical display.*

BELOW: *A large, scented candle sits on a crystal candlestick decorated with an elaborate wreath of paper flowers and wired beads.*
RIGHT: *Paper flowers and a large bow have been added to an antique silver candelabrum and candlesticks for this romantic table setting.*

Candles seem to be available in every high street in myriad colours, shapes and sizes. Whatever your wedding theme or style, you'll find candles to match, in shapes from fruits and flowers to cubes, pillars and spheres. Scented candles are popular but need to be used sensitively at a reception. Don't burn anything that will compete with the food you're serving, such as powerfully scented aromatherapy candles; you're safer with floral perfumes such as rose, jasmine or lily. Nightlights are the most economical option and can easily be bought in bulk. They're simple and unpretentious but, particularly when used on a grand scale, look enchanting. Church candles are a classic choice and lend themselves to elegant displays (such as the fireplace on page 22). Floating candles are ideal for table centrepieces and can often be found in pretty shapes such as

a glorious glow

stars, shells or flowers. You'll need tall, slender candles if you're using candlesticks or candelabra, and you may also come across very fine tapers which, like nightlights, look best when arranged en masse.

Decorative candle holders and containers serve the practical purpose of enclosing the flame. Traditional candlesticks and candelabra, whether crystal, china, silver or wrought iron, can be embellished with garlands of flowers or ivy, or lengths of beaded wire. Plain- or frosted-glass votives will enhance any setting. Homely versions can be made from jam jars, wrapped round with sheer fabric or thin paper to diffuse the light, or trimmed with ivy. Moroccan-style gilded tealights add glamour and cast pools of coloured light. Lanterns come in many guises and are a good choice for outdoors, shielding the flames from wind. They look magical at night edging a path or dotted along a wall.

If you want candles on your tables, tiny flickering votives or tealights are an obvious choice. For large-scale impact, group votives together on a tray or mirror (see pages 128–129). For table centrepieces, displays of floating

A B O V E : *White rice – which could be replaced with coffee beans, white pebbles or glass nuggets – holds chunky cream candles in place inside straight-sided glass bowls. For an outdoor reception, citronella candles and garden flares help to keep insects at bay.*

L E F T   A N D   O P P O S I T E : *Nightlights burn brightly in glass lanterns suspended at different heights with coloured ribbons.*
R I G H T : *Tiny votives trimmed with circles of ivy illuminate a path for guests.*

THIS PAGE: *These sleek modern candle holders can be filled with anything decorative — glass beads or flowers, perhaps. The addition of a name card has turned them into place markers.*

candles are safe and beautiful to look at and can be created in any sort of broad, shallow dish or bowl. Goldfish bowls look good, too, filled with flower heads, petals and floating candles. Candlesticks and candelabra work well on tables (see page 131), keeping flames safely raised and allowing guests to talk around them, but they're also tailor-made for displays on mantelpieces or side tables. Another approach to decorating a mantelpiece is to collect a number of candles and holders and arrange them as a glowing, atmospheric still life.

Candles look good indoors or out, whether a wedding is formal, traditional, modern or informal. Like flowers, they instantly create a celebratory and romantic atmosphere. Moreover, their beauty comes at a reasonable price, so – even if you buy no more than a few bags of nightlights – you'll be guaranteed your own enchanted evening.

Did you know THAT PURE BEESWAX CANDLES BURN CLEANER AND BRIGHTER THAN STANDARD CANDLES, DON'T DRIP OR SMOKE, AND LAST LONGER? AS WELL AS HAVING A SWEET AROMA, THEY PRODUCE NEGATIVE IONS AND THEREFORE HELP TO CLEAN THE AIR.

ABOVE: *For a winter wedding reception, paper leaves, handwritten with guests' names and table numbers, have been attached with wire to an ivy wreath that encircles a large, three-wick candle.*
RIGHT: *A pretty bow gives a fretwork lantern a festive air.*
FAR RIGHT: *White wire lanterns, hung with sparkling glass beads, hang from trees and shrubs in a summer garden.*

SOURCES

BRIDALWEAR AND BRIDESMAIDS' ATTIRE

DAVID CHARLES
CHILDRENSWEAR
2–4 Thane Works
Thane Villas
London N7 7NU
020 7609 4797
*Party and bridesmaid dresses
for 2–12 year olds.*

DEBENHAMS
Visit www.debenhams.com or call
08456 055 044 for stores that
carry the Bridalwear collection.
*Designer bridal gowns as well as
shoes, lingerie and bridesmaids'
and pageboys' outfits.*

HOUSE OF FRASER STORES
(Including Dickens & Jones)
Visit www.houseoffraser.com or
call 020 7963 2000 for details of
your nearest store.
*Designs for brides, bridesmaids
and pageboys*

K+K KIRSTEN ABERNETHY
07906 947 968
kirstenabernethy@yahoo.com.au
Bespoke dress designer.

MONSOON
Call 0870 412 9000 for details of
your local store.
*Off-the-peg wedding dresses and
outfits for bridesmaids up to 12
and pageboys up to 8 years.*

MORGAN DAVIES
62 Cross Street
London N1 2BA
020 7354 3414
www.morgandavies-london.co.uk
Modern wedding dresses.

VIRGIN BRIDES
35 King Street
Manchester M2 7AT
0870 0600 436
www.virginbrides.co.uk
*Bridalwear, adult bridesmaid's
dresses, and accessories.*

THE WEDDING PORTFOLIO,
INCLUDING SOIE MEME
76 Belsize Park Gardens
London NW3 4NG
Call 020 7483 3843 for
details of stockists.
www.soiememe.com
*Couture bridal gowns,
bridesmaids and pageboys.*

THE WEDDING SHOP
Liberty
Regent Street
London W1B 5AH
020 7573 9922
www.weddingshop.com
*European distributors of
bridalwear by Vera Wang, Elie
Saab and Carolina Herrera.*

SPECIALIST WEDDING STORE

CONFETTI
80–81 Tottenham Court Road,
London W1T 4TE
020 7436 7177
Visit www.confetti.co.uk or call
0870 840 6060 for enquiries and
mail order.

CAKES

**All the cakes featured in this
book were made by:**
SAVOIR DESIGN
The Garden House
2 Vardens Road
London SW11 1RH
020 8877 9770

www.savoirdesign.co.uk
*Exquisite wedding cakes
specially created by celebrity
pastry chef Eric Lanlard.*

Other cakemakers:
KONDITOR AND COOK
22 Cornwall Road
London SE1 8TW
www.konditorandcook.co.uk
*Unconventional wedding cakes
plus patisserie.*

LITTLE VENICE CAKE
COMPANY
15 Manchester Mews
London W1U 2DX
020 7486 5252
www.lvcc.co.uk
Bespoke wedding cakes.

THE LITTLE WEDDING CAKE
COMPANY
www.littlecakes.co.uk
*A range of personalized
miniature wedding cakes.*

CANDLES

PRICE'S CANDLES
100 York Road
London SW11 3RU
020 7924 6336
www.prices-candles.co.uk
*Fine quality candles of all
shapes, sizes and scents.*

CONFETTI

FOREVER MEMORIES
112 High Street
Kinver
Stourbridge
West Midlands DY7 6HL
01384 878 111
www.forevermemories.co.uk
*Metallic and paper confetti as
well as freeze-dried and fabric*

*rose petals. Also favour boxes
in varying shapes and sizes,
and personalized ribbon.*

PASSION FOR PETALS
Bougainvillea Limited
Box 22
Ottery St Mary
Devon EX11 1XE
01404 811 467
www.passionforpetals.com
*Bougainvillea petal confetti
in every shade of pink, as
well as freeze-dried rose petals.
Also flower seeds for use as
favours and round glass-topped
metallic favour cases.*

TRULY MADLY DEEPLY
Visit www.trulymadlydeeply.biz
or call 0870 120 0316
*Real flower petal confetti,
including rose petals, delphiniums
and lavender grains. Also
beaded candle surrounds and
personalized chocolate favours.*

FAVOURS

BOMBONIERE
Call 020 7636 1120 for
details of stockists.
www.chocolateplease.com

COLOGNE & COTTON
88 Marylebone High Street
London W1U 4QX
020 7486 0595
www.cologneandcotton.co.uk
*Lavender sachets and beautifully
packaged candles and scents.*

I LOVE YOU MORE THAN
CHOCOLATE
Visit www.iloveyoumorethan
chocolate.co.uk
or call 01373 830 013
Stylish chocolate favours.

PAPERCHASE
213 Tottenham Court Road
London W1T 7PS
Visit www.paperchase.co.uk
or call 020 7467 6200 for
details of your nearest store.
Giftwrap, place cards, confetti,
crackers and novelty items.

ROCOCO
321 Kings Road
London SW3 5EP
Visit www.rococochocolates.com
or call 020 7352 5857 for details
of stockists and their brochure.
Beautifully packaged chocolates,
truffles, nougats, etc.

THE VERY NICE COMPANY
www.theverynicecompany.com
Perspex containers, favour
boxes, lottery-ticket envelopes,
bags, bottles of bubbles, and
biodegradable confetti.

WITH LOVE FROM
www.withlovefrom.co.uk
Favour boxes, wedding-cake-
shaped candles, craft boxes
and fabric and paper gift bags.

GENERAL TABLETOP

GRANGE
74–75 Marylebone High Street
London W1U 5JW
020 7935 7000
www.grangelondon.co.uk
Decorative table accessories.

NORDIC STYLE
109 Lots Road
London SW10 ORN
020 7351 1755
www.nordicstyle.com
Antique-style Swedish
glassware, painted china, linen
and pewter candlesticks.

OKA
Visit www.okadirect.com
or call 0870 160 6002
for details of their mail-order
catalogue and the location
of their stores.
Decorative china, glassware,
candlesticks and fabric flowers.

THOMAS GOODE
19 South Audley Street
London W1K 2BN
020 7499 2823
www.thomasgoode.co.uk
China, silverware and glassware.
Wedding list service available.

TABLE LINEN

ANTIQUE DESIGNS LIMITED
Ash House
Ash House Lane
Little Leigh, Northwich
Cheshire CW8 4RG
01606 892822
www.antique-designs.co.uk
Antique-style luxury linens.

IRISH LINEN COMPANY
35–36 Burlington Arcade
London W1J 0QB
020 7493 8949
www.irish-linen.com
Fine Irish linen tablecloths
and napkins.

JANE SACCHI LINENS
020 7349 7020
Visit www.janesacchi.com
or call 020 7838 1001 for
details of mail order.
Antique bed and table linen.
Wedding list service available.

VOLGA LINEN
Visit www.volgalinen.co.uk
or call 01728 635020 for
details of stockists.

Linen tablecloths, napkins
and placemats in damasks,
plain weaves and drawn
thread work embroidery.

THE WHITE COMPANY
Visit www.thewhiteco.com
or call 0870 900 9555 for
details of their mail-order
catalogue and your nearest store.
Good value table linen and
table accessories.

CHINA AND GLASSWARE

BACCARAT
Available from:
Harrods
87–135 Brompton Road
London SW1X 7XL
020 7730 1234
www.baccarat.fr
Fine French crystal.

CHRISTOFLE UK LTD
10 Hanover Street
London W1S 1YG
020 7491 4004
www.christofle.com
Cutlery, fine porcelain,
crystal and silverware.
Wedding list service available.

DESIGNERS GUILD
267–271 Kings Road
London SW3 5EW
020 7893 7400
www.designersguild.com
Table linen in funky DG prints.

HABITAT UK
Visit www.habitat.net
or call 0845 6010740 for
details of your nearest store.
Inexpensive, stylish tableware.

HEREND PORCELAIN
4 Burlington Arcade
London W1J OPD

020 7629 9229
www.herend.com
Fine Hungarian porcelain.

IKEA
Visit www.IKEA.co.uk for
details of your nearest store.
Inexpensive, stylish tableware.

LALIQUE
162 Bond Street
London W1Y 9PA
020 7499 8228
www.lalique.com
Fine French porcelain, china
and stemware.

RENWICK & CLARKE
TRADING LTD
The Old Imperial Laundry
71 Warriner Gardens
London SW11 4 XW
020 7720 0311
www.renwickandclarke.com
China, cutlery and glassware.

RICHARD GINORI
Distributed in UK by ICTC
3 Caley Close
Sweet Briar Road
Norwich NR3 2BU
01603 488019
www.ictc.co.uk
Italian porcelain.

ROYAL WORCESTER
Severn Street
Worcester WR1 2NE
Visit www.royal-worcester.co.uk
or call 01905 746000 for
details of your nearest stockist.

WEDGWOOD
Visit www.wedgwood.com
or call 0800 028 0026 for
details of your nearest stockist.
Fine bone china by
Kelly Hoppen, Jasper Conran,
and Paul Costelloe.

WILLIAM YEOWARD CRYSTAL
336 Kings Road
London SW3 5UR
020 7351 5454
www.williamyeowardcrystal.com
*Crystal inspired by antique
pieces originally made in
England and Ireland during the
18th and early 19th centuries.*

WATERFORD CRYSTAL
Visit www.waterford.com
or call 0800 039 0077 for
details of your nearest stockist.
*Stemware collections from
John Rocha and Jasper Conran.*

CUTLERY/FLATWARE

GLAZEBROOK & CO.
020 7731 7135
www.glazebrook.com
*British stainless-steel cutlery
in classic designs.*

ROBERT WELCH
Lower High Street
Chipping Campden
Gloucestershire GL55 6DY
Visit www.welch.co.uk or call
01386 840522 for stockists.
*Silverware, tableware and
glassware. Wedding list
service available.*

ROBBE & BERKING
Available at Herend Porcelain
(as above)
Fine German silverware.

DECORATIVE ACCESSORIES

BEAD SHOP
Creative Beadcraft Ltd
20 Beak Street
London W1F 9RE
www.creativebeadcraft.co.uk

*Beads, sequins, trimmings,
pearls, diamante and more.*

EVERTRADING
Visit www.evertrading.co.uk
or call 020 8878 4050 for
details of your nearest
stockist or their mail-order
catalogue.

FENWICK
63 New Bond Street
London W1A 3BS
020 7629 9161
www.fenwick.co.uk
Stylish accessories.

FIGARO INTERIORS LIMITED
293 Fulham Road
London SW10 9PZ
020 7352 0260
www.figarointeriors.co.uk
*Stockists of the Sia range
of candle holders, napkin
holders, cake stands and
silk flowers.*

JOHN LEWIS
Visit www.johnlewis.com for
details of your nearest store.
*Decorative haberdashery,
including beads, pearl-headed
pins, ribbons and feathers.*

INDIA JANE
131–133 King's Road
London SW3 4PW
020 7351 1060
*Glassware, candles and
ceramics.*

JOANNA WOOD
48a Pimlico Road
London SW1W 8LP
020 7730 5064
www.joannawood.com
*Quirky gifts ideal for tabletop
decoration or as favours.*

MENU A/S
Kongevejen 2
DK 3480 Fredensborg
Denmark
00 45 48 40 61 00
www.menuas.com
Sleek modern tableware.

V.V. ROULEAUX
6 Marylebone High Street
London W1U 4NJ
020 7224 5179
www.vvrouleaux.com
*Ribbons and decorative
accessories.*

SPINA DESIGN
Robbie Spina and Joe Zito
Visit www.spinadesign.co.uk
or call 020 7328 5274.
*Luxurious, hand-made
trimmings, tassels and tiebacks.*

STYLE ISLAND
Visit www.styleisland.com
or call 01373 812223.
*Stylish tableware, small gifts,
jewellery and food and drink.*

WEMYSS-HOULES LTD
40–44 Newman Street
London W1T 1QD
020 7255 3305
Trims and trimmings.

OUTDOOR ACCESSORIES

R.K. ALLISTON
173 New Kings Road
London SW6 4SW
020 7751 0077
www.rkalliston.com
*Citronella candles in terracotta
pots, glass and paper lanterns.*

KENNETH TURNER
59 South Molton Street
London W1Y 1HH
020 7409 2560

www.kennethturner.com
*Fresh flowers and potted plants,
home and garden accessories.*

MARSTON & LANGINGER
192 Ebury Street
London SW1W 8UP
020 7881 5717
www.marston-and-langinger.com
*Wrought iron and wirework
chandeliers and hurricane
lamps. Pots, baskets and
glassware.*

FABRICS

LELIEVRE
Chelsea Harbour Design Centre
London SW10 OXE
Call 020 7352 4798 for
details of your local stockist.

JANE CHURCHILL
151 Sloane Street
London SW1 X9B
020 7730 9847
Call 020 8874 6484 for
details of your nearest stockist.

FURNITURE
AND FURNITURE HIRE

PARTY LINEN
www.partylinen.co.uk
*Chair covers for hire, as
well as props for wedding
receptions, including
topiary trees, stone
urns and candelabras.*

PURVES & PURVES
222 Tottenham Court Road
London W1T 7PZ
020 7580 8223
www.purves.co.uk
*Retailers of white Arne Jacobsen
style 'Phoenix' chairs.*

RAYNERS

Catering Equipment Hire
Banquet House
118–120 Garratt Lane
London SW18 4DJ
020 8870 6000
www.rayners.co.uk
Both traditional and contemporary
seating, glassware, china, cake
stands and table linen to hire.

SPACEWORKS

Visit www.spaceworks.co.uk
or call 0800 854 486.
Traditional wedding chairs
in many colours as well as
garden benches, parasols
and other outdoor furniture.

STATIONERY

THE LETTER PRESS
OF CIRENCESTER

3–9 Cripps Road
Cirencester
Gloucestershire GL7 1HN
01285 659797
www.letterpress.co.uk
Traditional high-quality bespoke
wedding stationery, available
from branches of the
John Lewis Partnership.

SMYTHSON

40 New Bond Street
London W1S 2DE
020 7629 8558
www.smythson.com
Bespoke wedding stationery.

THE WREN PRESS

1 Chelsea Wharf
15 Lots Road
London SW10 0QJ
020 7351 5887
www.wrenpress.com
Fine wedding stationery.

WEDDING VENUES

28 PORTLAND PLACE

28 Portland Place
London W1B 1DE
020 7653 6666
www.28portlandplace.co.uk

NOBLES VENUES

www.noblesvenues.com
Venues for all kinds of
events, functions and
activities, especially
weddings and parties.

SYON LODGE
& GARDENS

Busch Corner
London Road
Middlesex TW7 5BH
020 8847 1732
www.syonlodgeandgardens.co.uk

PICTURE CREDITS

All photography by Polly Wreford

Endpapers favour boxes from Confetti, striped ribbons from V V Rouleaux; **2** 28 Portland Place, London/gold-rimmed glasses, silver rose bowl and cutlery all from Thomas Goode, crystal jug from William Yeoward Crystal, gold-rimmed table setting from Royal Worcester; **3 inset** candles from Price's Candles, silver beaded candle holder from V V Rouleaux; **4l** Skywood House, Middlesex designed by architect Graham Phillips/spotty ribbon from VV Rouleaux, silver-edge china from Royal Worcester; **4c** hand-made paper from Paperchase, wire mesh butterflies from Confetti; **4r** pressed glass plates and cutlery from Marston & Langinger; **5** Skywood House, Middlesex designed by architect Graham Phillips; **6-7** Syon Lodge & Gardens, Isleworth, London; **6** floral china table setting from Richard Ginori, engraved goblet set from Evertrading, silver shallow vase from Kenneth Turner, chairs from Nordic Style; **7br** crystal wine glasses from William Yeoward Crystal, purple chiffon ribbon from V V Rouleaux; **8** (clockwise) wire-rimmed flower, miniature white beads, white silk and flower beaded ribbons, gold striped and spotty ribbons all from V V Rouleaux, mother of pearl dance card holder from Antique Designs Ltd, gold foil heart-shaped chocolate and sugared almonds from Rococo, faux white rose from John Lewis, white beads '2' from the Bead Shop, (centre) white card and envelope from Paperchase, gold heart-shaped sparklers and paper bag with sequinned flower from Confetti; **9** heart-shaped lavender ring cushion from Nordic Style; **10** embroidered cloth hanger from Cologne & Cotton, sequinned flower ribbon and artificial flower bushel from V V Rouleaux, embroidered fabric from Lelievre; **11a** lamp and chair from Purves & Purves, stationery, notebooks and pens from Paperchase, white plastic file holders from Muji; **11b** (clockwise) braided pink ribbon with flowers (Braid JM 20E-02) from Jane Churchill, faux pink flower from Figaro Interiors, blue and white spotty fabric from Jane Churchill, beaded bag from Confetti, blue sequinned flower from V V Rouleaux, picture/place card holder from Confetti, lilac stationery and blue flower strips from Paperchase, striped blue and white fabric with pink flowers (J26oF) from Jane Churchill; **12-13l** handmade stationery, notebooks and

albums from Paperchase; **13r** multi-coloured file holders from Rymans; **14-17** Skywood House, Middlesex designed by architect Graham Phillips; **14al** white silk dress from Monsoon; **14bl** John Rocha etched wine glasses from Waterford Crystal; **14r** tall tapered glass vase from Habitat, stainless steel and glass candle and menu holders from Menu A/S; **15** chairs from Purves & Purves; **16-17l** Jasper Conran plates available at Wedgwood, cutlery from IKEA, damask napkins from Volga Linen; **17c** 3-tiered cake decorated with icing pearls designed by Eric at Savoir Design; **17r** heart-shaped mould ice cube tray from IKEA, glass ice bucket from John Lewis; **18-21** Syon Lodge & Gardens, Isleworth, London; **18** fold-up garden chairs from Habitat, flowered fabric with sylvan stripe on chairs from Jane Churchill; **19l** coloured wine glass from Thomas Goode, Sia faux flowers from Figaro Interiors, spiral plate from Designers Guild; **19r** candy pink favour box from Paperchase, ribbon from V V Rouleaux, floral gold-rimmed plates from Royal Worcester; **20al** Chinese lanterns from IKEA; **20bl** gilt-edged cake stand from Kenneth Turner, favour boxes from Confetti; **21l** cream painted wire baskets from Fenwick; **21r** etched crystal goblets from Evertrading, spiral plates from Designers Guild, damask tablecloth from Antique Linen Company, pink and blue damask napkins from Thomas Goode; **22-25** 28 Portland Place, London; **22l** large church candles from Price's Candles; **23** silver rose bowl, cream napkins and gilt hoop napkin holders from Thomas Goode, gold-rimmed china from Royal Worcester, crystal jug from William Yeoward Crystal; **24** gold-rimmed glasses and cutlery from Thomas Goode, gold and white china from Royal Worcester; **25l** silver rose bowl from Thomas Goode; **25c** gold and white china from Royal Worcester; **26al** favour boxes from Bomboniere, crystal wine glass and flower vase from William Yeoward Crystal; **26ar** fold-up garden chair from Habitat; **27** patterned china from Richard Ginori, crystal glassware from William Yeoward Crystal, cutlery from Oka, wire beaded garland table decoration from V V Rouleaux, damask tablecloth from Antique Designs Ltd; **28r** coloured crystal wine glass from William Yeoward Crystal; **29** see p 27 for details; **30 & 31r**

bridesmaid's dress designed by David Charles; **31l** white silk dress from Monsoon; **32l** vintage kimono apron top designed by K+K, pink and green flower fabric braid from Jane Churchill; **32c** white silk dress from Monsoon; **33** beaded bracelet from VV Rouleaux; **36-37** Skywood House, Middlesex designed by architect Graham Phillips; **36** 3-tiered cake decorated with icing pearls designed by Eric at Savoir Design, pink satin ribbon from V V Rouleaux; **37l-c** pink satin dress from House of Fraser; **39-40** 28 Portland Place, London; **40-41** all ribbons from V V Rouleaux, pearl-headed dressmaker's pins from John Lewis; **42c** patterned umbrella fabric from Lelievre; **42r** flower girl's dress from Monsoon, flowered handbag from Dickens & Jones; **43** braided fabric and pearl-headed dressmaker's pins from John Lewis; **44-45** patterned umbrella fabric from Lelievre, red and blue passementerie from Wemyss Houles, flowery braided pink ribbon sash (JM20E) from Jane Churchill; **45bc** bridesmaid's dress designed by David Charles; **46b** embroidered tray cloth from Antique Designs Ltd; **47** embroidered table linen from the Irish Linen Company; **49r** heart-shaped wooden tray from Nordic Style; **50** Skywood House, Middlesex designed by architect Graham Phillips/etched goblets from Oka, cutlery from IKEA; **51l** china from Royal Worcester, stemmed glasses from Habitat, cutlery from IKEA; **51c** china from Richard Ginori; **51r** shot glasses from Habitat; **52** Skywood House, Middlesex designed by architect Graham Phillips/cups and saucers from Wedgwood, similar cylindrical flower vase available from IKEA and Habitat, blue-rimmed china from Royal Worcester, 4-tiered cake from Savoir Design; **53c** cream pot and wire-hooped plants from The Netherlands Flower Bulb Information Centre; **53r** Jasper Conran plates available at Wedgwood, cutlery from Glazebrook & Company, glassware from Stuart Crystal, cream and white pots and all plants from The Netherlands Flower Bulb Information Centre; **55** 28 Portland Place, London; **55bl** cutlery and pot from Christofle UK Ltd, crystal wine glass from Evertrading; **56-57** flower glass vase from Evertrading; **58l** 28 Portland Place, London; **58c, r & 59** Syon Lodge & Gardens, Isleworth, London; **59** chairs and cushions from Nordic Style; **60**

140 PICTURE CREDITS

INDEX

Figures in italics indicate captions.

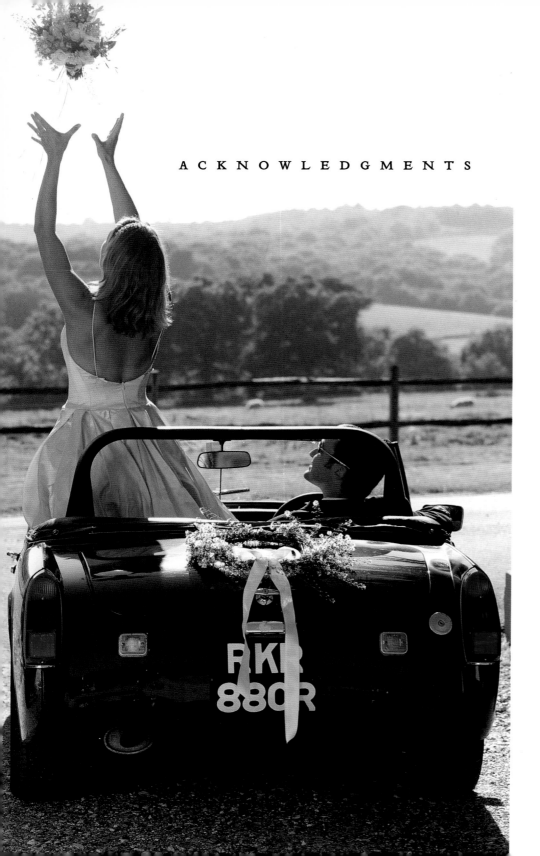

ACKNOWLEDGMENTS

My very special thanks go to the 'team' – to my assistant Paul Hopper for creating such lovely bridal bouquets and wedding presents and for his constant cheerful support; to our brilliant and inspired photographer, the lovely Polly Wreford, for capturing romance in every picture; to our talented art director, Gabriella Le Grazie, for all her enthusiastic 'Loverlys!' and for always joining in and helping us. My thanks too to Catherine Griffin, Pamela Daniels and Matt Wrixon, for all their help and for posing as brides and groom; Claire Hector for finding such unusual locations; Chris Mills (Man on the Move) for safely transporting our wedding props from place to place; Biddy Akerman at Special Flower Projects for her romantic country flowers; Makiko Sakita at Confetti for lending us the beautiful wedding cake she made; Eric at Savoir Designs for creating the wedding cakes we wanted to eat but never could; Kate French at *Brides* magazine for all her invaluable help; a big thank you to my friend Jill Koerner for sewing for us at the eleventh hour; and my agent Fiona Lindsay at Limelight.

Also, I must thank all the stores who loaned us merchandise for photography – particularly Annabelle Lewis at V V Rouleaux, Thomas Goode, the staff at Confetti, Richard Ginori for lending so many beautiful sets of china, and Jenny at William Yeoward Crystal.

However, my extra-special thanks and appreciation go to three wonderful children – Hector, Caspar and Celia Fraser – who made the ultimate sacrifice of missing bathtime, not doing homework and staying up late to model in our photographs.

Thank you all very much,

MC